THE SHOOTING SCRIPT

SYNECDOCHE, NEW YORK

THE SHOOTING SCRIPT

SYNECDOCHE, NEW YORK

Screenplay and Introduction by Charlie Kaufman

A Newmarket Shooting Script® Series Book
NEWMARKET PRESS • NEW YORK

Screenplay, photographs, and cover artwork copyright © 2008 Kimmel Distribution, LLC. All rights reserved.

Introduction copyright © 2008 by Charlie Kaufman

Q&A copyright © 2008 by Rob Feld

All rights reserved. Used by permission.

The Newmarket Shooting Script® Series is a registered trademark of Newmarket Publishing & Communications Company.

This book is published simultaneously in the United States of America and in Canada.

All rights reserved. This book may not be reproduced, in whole or in part, in any form, without written permission. Inquiries should be addressed to: Permissions Department, Newmarket Press, 18 East 48th Street, New York, NY 10017.

FIRST EDITION

10 9 8 7 6 5 4 3 2 1

ISBN-13: 978-1-55704-813-4

Library of Congress Catalog-in-Publication Data available upon request.

QUANTITY PURCHASES

Companies, professional groups, clubs, and other organizations may qualify for special terms when ordering quantities of this title. For information, write to Special Sales, Newmarket Press, 18 East 48th Street, New York, NY 10017; call (212) 832-3575 or 1-800-669-3903; FAX (212) 832-3629; or e-mail info@newmarketpress.com.

Website: www.newmarketpress.com

Manufactured in the United States of America.

OTHER BOOKS IN THE NEWMARKET SHOOTING SCRIPT® SERIES INCLUDE:

About a Boy: The Shooting Script	The Ice Storm: The Shooting Script
Adaptation: The Shooting Script	Little Miss Sunshine: The Shooting Script
The Age of Innocence: The Shooting Script	Margot at the Wedding: The Shooting Script
American Beauty: The Shooting Script	The Matrix: The Shooting Script
A Beautiful Mind: The Shooting Script	Michael Clayton: The Shooting Script
The Birdcage: The Shooting Script	The People vs. Larry Flynt: The Shooting Script
Black Hawk Down: The Shooting Script	Pieces of April: The Shooting Script
Capote: The Shooting Script	Punch-Drunk Love: The Shooting Script
Cinderella Man: The Shooting Script	The Savages: The Shooting Script
The Constant Gardener: The Shooting Script	The Shawshank Redemption: The Shooting Script
Dan in Real Life: The Shooting Script	Sideways: The Shooting Script
Dead Man Walking: The Shooting Script	Snow Falling on Cedars: The Shooting Script
Eternal Sunshine of the Spotless Mind: The Shooting Script	The Squid and the Whale: The Shooting Script
	State and Main: The Shooting Script
Gods and Monsters: The Shooting Script	Stranger Than Fiction: The Shooting Script
Gosford Park: The Shooting Script	Traffic: The Shooting Script
Human Nature: The Shooting Script	Transamerica: The Shooting Script
Juno: The Shooting Script	The Truman Show: The Shooting Script
Knocked Up: The Shooting Script	War of the Worlds: The Shooting Script

OTHER NEWMARKET PICTORIAL MOVIEBOOKS AND NEWMARKET INSIDER FILM BOOKS INCLUDE:

The Art of The Matrix*	Hotel Rwanda: Bringing the True Story of an African Hero to Film*
The Art of X2*	The Kite Runner: A Portrait of the Marc Forster Film*
The Art of X-Men: The Last Stand	The Jaws Log
Bram Stoker's Dracula: The Film and the Legend*	Memoirs of a Geisha: A Portrait of the Film
Chicago: The Movie and Lyrics*	The Mummy: Tomb of the Dragon Emperor
Dances with Wolves: The Illustrated Story of the Epic Film*	Ray: A Tribute to the Movie, the Music, and the Man*
Dreamgirls	Rush Hour: Lights, Camera, Action
E.T. The Extra-Terrestrial: From Concept to Classic*	Saving Private Ryan: The Men, The Mission, The Movie
Gladiator: The Making of the Ridley Scott Epic Film	Schindler's List: Images of the Steven Spielberg Film
Good Night, and Good Luck: The Screenplay and History Behind the Landmark Movie*	Superbad: The Illustrated Moviebook*
	Tim Burton's Corpse Bride: An Invitation to the Wedding

*Includes Screenplay

CONTENTS

Introduction by Charlie Kaufman	vii
The Shooting Script	1
Stills	following page 82
Q & A with Charlie Kaufman	133
Cast and Crew Credits	153
About the Screenwriter/Director	161

INTRODUCTION

BY CHARLIE KAUFMAN

They want me to write an introduction to this thing. They're pestering me. This guy, Keith, at Newmarket Press. I've already consented to and gone through a long interview for this book and am currently mired in endless press for the movie, which opens soon enough but not soon enough for me. I'm traveling the country (San Francisco, Boston, New York, D.C., Chicago, Dallas, Austin, Denver, Seattle—I think that's it) and back and forth twice to Europe in the month of October alone. On a plane almost every night for the entire month. So on top of that, they keep asking me to do this introduction thing and I keep saying, through intermediaries, that I don't have the time or the inclination. I just got a new e-mail, just now, right now, from Keith, saying they left a space at the beginning of the book for my introduction, as if my responses never got to them. So, okay, now I'm writing this version, sort of out of spite. I don't get any money for these books. There's a screenplay book for each of my produced movies. I think I got one eight-dollar check once. So I'm not motivated and a little pissy.

    The other thing is they have the idea that I really need to explain in an introduction why I chose to publish this version of the screenplay, the one in the book you're holding, if anyone is holding this. Is anyone holding this? The thing is it doesn't seem that interesting a topic. But okay, if anyone cares, I chose this version because I had to choose some version and this version was the easiest to prepare because it is basically the version we went into production with; it's already put together. If I were to have to put together a version based on the finished film, I would have had to deal with the changes that came about during production and editing: improvised lines, rewrites, new voice-overs, switched-around scene order, blah blah blah, which I don't have the time for or the interest in doing. I don't want to have to read this script again, let alone reconstruct it. I'm really just trying to get through this process; the finish line is almost visible. Nobody ever buys these things, anyway. I'm not even sure why they're published. I think it's more or less a promotional tool for the theatrical release of the movie. So on every movie, I have the exact same discussion with the producer. It goes:

Him: What do you want to do about the screenplay book?
Me: I don't care. Let's not do it.
Him: (slightly judgmental pause) I think we should. Should we go with Esther [publisher at Newmarket]? She loves the movie.
Me: I don't care. That's fine.
Him: Okay. Which draft should we use?
Me: I don't care. Whatever is easiest.
Him: (slightly judgmental pause) Okay.
Me: (slightly defensive, slightly pleading) I mean, what difference does it make?
Him: Okay. I'll let them know.

So here I am, as I knew I would be once I agreed to having this thing published, trying to write an introduction and being mad at Keith. I don't even know Keith. I've never seen him, as far as I know, which may be completely untrue. I may have met him forty times and not paid attention. I don't even know his job title, that's how much Keith and this screenplay book are part of my life. Every movie I write I'm asked to participate in the making of these books. I think with *Being John Malkovich* it was kind of exciting for me. It was my first script and it was getting published. But I soon learned that nobody buys these things and nobody reads these things and I make no money from these things. So I started to get pissy about being approached at the end of each of these projects by people wanting to get me to work for free on a side project that would never be looked at by anyone. Who is Keith that he should have the right to badger me so? I don't know. I would guess he's forty. I guess he sits in an office. Maybe he has blond hair parted neatly on the side. Wears glasses? That's kind of it. Mostly he's a pest to me, not part of my life, not interesting. When I see his e-mails on my computer, I find myself feeling angry and put upon. He's an annoyance to me. That is all he is. But if I stop and think about it, which I just did, if I try to broaden my view of the world, which I just did, I realize that every moment I exist as me, Keith exists as Keith. He is not the occasional letter in my e-mail box. Every moment of every day, he is living a life somewhere far away from me. As an experiment, I decided to e-mail Keith and ask him to tell me a bit about himself. After questioning my intentions ("Hey, Charlie—you poking fun at me or what?"), followed by my brief response assuring him I was not ("not poking fun—it's a real idea I'm toying with"), Keith sent me this:

"Okay—I'll answer your broad questions below very quickly and hope that it gives you a springboard for your piece. I'm going to be very upfront. You know you have set out Caden's life in an incredibly sweeping way, so here's a quick stab at mine.

"I grew up in the '50s in a sheltered, supposedly idyllic setting in Connecticut, watching my father trudge off to Manhattan every morning and vowing that would not be my plight. We'd enjoy toast and tea in the morning, and then I'd wave him off.

"In the '60s I attended a prestigious boys' prep school in Massachusetts that totally radicalized me—rebelling against the ancient ways of tradition there, I began publishing an underground paper, writing poetry, protesting against the war in Vietnam. I opted for Oberlin College in faraway Ohio for college, and that was a paradise—the place was alive with women (!), lively thought, music, paintings, movies galore, politics, spiritual studies (I studied with a Tibetan monk named Geshe Sopa, who taught meditation and a whole way of approaching life I longed for), so many interesting souls—including Julie Taymor and Bill Irwin. I fell into a romantic relationship of twelve years with a dancer. We moved to dreaded Manhattan and lived happily (for a while) on the Upper West Side. I had learned to hand-set books in Oberlin in the cold basement of an English professor, and four of us poets hand-printed tiny volumes that we were enormously proud of and realized that we could get out a different written word.

"I knew I wanted to be in publishing and after a hilarious stint at a vanity publishing operation, I landed an incredible job at Random House, working on the unabridged dictionary, finding new words and writing definitions. I continued at Random House for ten years and moved over to

Newmarket Press way back in 1989, a smaller company where I could be involved in every aspect of book making and publishing again.

"In the meantime I had a traumatic breakup with my college girlfriend and eventually started a long relationship with a Norwegian woman, also in publishing. She was very interested in spiritual studies as well and led me into the Gurdjieff studies, which would eventually take me to France, Switzerland, and back to New York. I lost Sandy to ovarian cancer in 1995, after her diagnosis in '91. She made a tremendous effort at healing herself, and that experience has informed the rest of my life.

"A year later I was blessed with meeting an amazing Japanese woman at a retreat in Phoenicia, New York, whom I ended up marrying at City Hall on the spur of the moment six months later, ostensibly to solve a visa problem, but an amazing love had manifested itself! I now have two stepsons, Nobu and Akira, and two granddaughters, Himuka and Minato, who just visited us. I don't speak Japanese very well, but it's been like entering another world altogether. It can be very sweet and seductive.

"I live 60 miles north of New York City now, in Brewster, New York, on a couple of acres with a pond—happily joined by an absolutely faithful mutt we adopted, along with three cats: Mei-chan from Yokohama, who requires Japanese food; Musashi, a toughie rescued from Brooklyn, who the vet said was male and hence the samurai name, but turns out she's female and still tough; and our newest member, Ikkyu, named after a Zen monk, a cat who crawled out of a blizzard last year and declared he had found his home.

"Recent anecdote: I no longer eat beef, but my dog relishes it. He comes out back with me where the grill is and keeps an eye on my cooking. Three days ago I pull off the cover to the grill and notice something under the grill—it's a mouse who's made a fantastic bed out of the cottony material that lines the grill cover and some leaves. I shoo her away and finally see that there are two newly born mice under her in this exquisite bed. The dog is excited, barking, and my wife comes out to see the family. We cover up the grill, wish them well, and cook the steak for the dog inside, seasoned just the way he likes it. I'll have to check on the mice one of these days to clean up their deserted nest.

"I love working on the books and drag the work around with me everywhere. I am driven by some crazy sense of perfection, which can never actually be attained, but it colors my day at work. I like the idea of the Middle Eastern master carpetmaker who intentionally introduces a tiny, seemingly insignificant flaw into the weaving to show his own humility to the unobtainable Spirit of Perfection.

"So today I have the remnants of a nasty head cold and a bit of a headache, but I've enjoyed writing this sweeping bio for you and hope it sparks whatever you might be looking for."

Wow. Keith's letter did way more than I anticipated. Now I love Keith. Now I feel a connection with him. There are so many things I love about Keith's letter. Not the least of which is his willingness to participate and his openness in talking about himself, his leap of faith that I would not abuse the confidence. I love that he took me seriously. It made me think: How many hundreds of people have worked on this film whom I've never had a conversation with, whom I don't know at all, didn't think it was important to know? There is no periphery, it seems. Periphery is an illusion of individual consciousness. Each of us in our own mind is the center of the universe, and everything falls off in direct relation to its proximity or importance to us. But if you move to the periphery of your own existence, you find it to be the center of someone else's. Now I feel a responsibility to Keith. I can't dismiss him anymore. I'm not sure I like that. Maybe it's easier to see people as peripheral. Maybe that's why we do it. It's a weird and daunting experience to let other people in their fullness into our minds. It is so much easier to see them as serving a purpose in our own lives.

In any event, this somehow seems to lead me to some of the things explored in the screenplay that you, imaginary person, are holding in your hands right now. And the relentlessly experienced life of yours that has brought you to this book at this time will now perhaps interact with the relentlessly experienced life of mine as it is represented by this script. I hope we recognize each other.

—Charlie Kaufman and Keith Hollaman
Los Angeles and New York, respectively

Synecdoche, New York

by

Charlie Kaufman

Master White Script March 12, 2007
Blue Revision (Full Script) April 27, 2007
Pink Revision May 18, 2007

A1 INT. CADEN AND ADELE'S BEDROOM - FALL 2005 - MORNING A1

   Darkness. The sound of a radio and pots and pans clanging fades in. Caden, 40, opens his eyes in bed, and groggily looks at himself in the bureau mirror. The bedside clock reads 7:45.

1 INT. CADEN AND ADELE'S KITCHEN - FALL 2005 - SAME 1

   Adele, 40, in t-shirt and sweats, mixes a bowl of instant oatmeal, puts it in the microwave.

                    RADIO VOICE
               ... a Labor Day luncheon today --

        OLIVE (O.S.)   RADIO VOICE
   Mommy! Done!   -- at Stuckey Hall --

              ADELE   RADIO VOICE
   Okay!   -- in downtown Schenectady --

   Adele leaves the kitchen. Caden, also 40, enters as she's leaving. He's dressed in a ratty terrycloth robe.

              CADEN   ADELE
   Morning.   Morning. Tried not to wake
                                   you.

                         CADEN
               Thanks. You didn't. I was just --

   As Caden's voice goes under, we follow Adele into --

2 INT. CADEN AND ADELE'S BATHROOM - FALL 2005 - CONTINUOUS 2

   Olive, 4, sits on the toilet. Adele enters, rips some toilet paper off the roll and proceeds to wipe Olive. The phone rings in the kitchen.

              ADELE   CADEN (O.S.)
   Caden, could you get that?   It's Maria. I don't want to.

                         ADELE
               Ugh. Caden!
                    (looks at bright green
                     smear on toilet paper)
               That's weird.

   The phone stops ringing.

                         OLIVE
               Is something wrong with my poop?

(CONTINUED)

CONTINUED:

<table>
<tr><td>ADELE
No, honey. It's just green.
Maybe you ate something
green.</td><td>MARIA'S VOICE
Hi, it's me. Where are you?
I'll try you on your cell.</td></tr>
</table>

              OLIVE (CONT'D)
    I didn't! What's wrong with me?!

A cellphone rings in the other room.

              ADELE
    Honey, I have to get this. You're
    going to be fine.

              OLIVE
    But, Mommy --

Adele runs into --

INT. CADEN AND ADELE'S KITCHEN - FALL 2005 - CONTINUOUS

She rifles through her purse, grabs her cellphone, answers.

              ADELE
    Hey.
        (laughing)
    Oh, wiping Olive's ass. You?

Caden is pouring himself a cup of coffee. He sips it and stares out the window. It's raining.

            ADELE (CONT'D)
    You're kidding! Holy fuck!

Caden exits with his coffee, annoyed about the phone call.

              CADEN
    I don't feel well.

INT. CADEN AND ADELE'S BATHROOM - FALL 2005 - CONTINUOUS

Caden passes the bathroom. Olive is staring into the toilet bowl. Adele can be heard chatting in the background.

              OLIVE
    Daddy, my poop is green.

Caden enters the bathroom, looks into the bowl at the green feces and smeared toilet paper. He seems freaked out.

            OLIVE (CONT'D)
    Am I going to be okay?

(CONTINUED)

CONTINUED:

      CADEN
   Of course, honey.

      OLIVE
   Did you have green poop when you
   were little?

    CADEN   OLIVE
I'm sure I did, honey.   Am I going to die?

    CADEN   OLIVE
Of course not. You probably I didn't! I didn't eat
ate something --   green!

      CADEN
   It'll be fine, sweetie. I'll be
   back in a minute.

      OLIVE (O.C.)
    (calling)
   Is poop alive?

EXT. CADEN AND ADELE'S HOUSE - FALL 2005 - MORNING

Caden steps out the front door in his bare feet and hurries down the driveway in the rain. He picks up the newspaper, pulls the mail from the box. As he heads back inside, he flips through the mail. There's a magazine called <u>Attending to your Illness</u> addressed to Caden. A diseased person on the cover. Across the street a gaunt man watches Caden, unseen.

INT. CADEN AND ADELE'S KITCHEN - FALL 2005 - MORNING

Caden sits at the kitchen table with his coffee, reading the paper, dated Friday, October 14, 2005.

      ADELE
   All right, baby. See you then.

Adele clicks off her cellphone.

      CADEN
   Harold Pinter died!

    ADELE   CADEN
Yeah? Huh. Well, he was   Oh wait. He won the Nobel
old, right?   Prize. Good for him.

      OLIVE (O.S.)
   Mom!

(CONTINUED)

CONTINUED:

ADELE
What?!

OLIVE (O.S.)
Do you need to come look at my poop again?!

ADELE
No, Olive, it's fine. Just flush.

OLIVE (O.S.)
What if it's alive? What if I kill it? It's green! Like plants!

ADELE
It's not alive, honey.

CADEN
God, remember that production of The Dumbwaiter I did at Albanyfest?

The toilet is flushed.

OLIVE (O.S.) (CONT'D)
Everything's alive. Everything grows big. That's how you know.

Olive enters.

ADELE
I have your oatmeal, honey.

OLIVE
I want peanut butter and jelly.

ADELE
Olive, c'mon. You told me oatmeal. This isn't a restaurant.

OLIVE
I don't want oatmeal.

Adele growls, grabs the oatmeal, dumps it in the sink.

OLIVE (CONT'D)
Sorry, Mommy! I'm sorry!

CADEN
(looking at paper)
They found Avian flu in Turkey. In the country Turkey not turkeys. It's in chickens.

Adele is making a peanut butter sandwich for Olive.

OLIVE (CONT'D)
Can I watch TV till school?

Caden clicks the remote for Olive and goes back to his paper. A cartoon cow talks to a cartoon sheep.

(CONTINUED)

                         COW
              There is a secret, something at
              play under the surface, growing
              like an invisible virus of thought.

The sheep nods. Caden pours himself some more coffee, opens
the milk carton to pour some in, then sniffs at the spout.
He checks the date on the carton. It's October 20.

           CADEN   COW
Man. Milk's expired. Jesus.   But you are being changed by
                               it. Second by second. Every
                               breath counts off time.

Caden goes back to his paper. Adele puts a peanut butter
sandwich in front of Olive.

                         ADELE
              Here. Now you better eat this.

           OLIVE   CADEN
I will.   The first black graduate of
                               the University of Alabama
                               died. Vivian Malone Jones.
                               Stroke. Only 63.

Adele stares out the window at the rain.

INT. DENTIST'S OFFICE - FALL 2005 - DAY

Caden is in the dentist's chair, a bloody bib around his
neck. The dentist, in surgical mask, probes his open mouth,
calls out numbers to an assistant, who records them.

                         DENTIST
              2, 2, 1. 3, 4, 2. 3, 4, 4.
                   (to Caden)
              Family coming for Thanksgiving?

INT. CADEN AND ADELE'S BATHROOM - WINTER 2005 - NIGHT

Caden shaves. A faucet explodes and smacks him in the
forehead. He is sent staggering backwards with a yelp, into
the far wall, his razor flying and blood pouring from a
jagged cut above his right eyebrow. Off-screen, we hear the
pounding footsteps of someone running toward us. Half of
Caden's face is covered with shaving cream. Rivulets of
blood intermingle with it. Water shoots out where the tap
was, spraying the mirror, which is spattered with blood.
Adele, dressed in heavily paint-splattered clothes, hurries
in and takes in the scene: the wet, the mess, the blood.

                                                  (CONTINUED)

CONTINUED:

ADELE
Jesus! Caden! What the fuck -- ?!

Olive, in a nightgown, stands quietly in the doorway, her curled toes clenched. She holds a large stuffed owl.

CADEN
Um. I was shaving and --

ADELE
My God! Jesus! Look at your head!

Dumbly, Caden tries to look up at his forehead, then squints nervously at himself in the mirror.

ADELE (CONT'D)
(to Olive)
Honey, don't look.

Olive turns around.

ADELE (CONT'D)
Put pressure. Press. Press!

CADEN
Do I press above or below it?

ADELE
I don't know! Just... both!

Caden sits on the toilet, presses a towel to his head. Adele squats, goes into a spasmodic coughing fit, finishes, opens the cabinet under the sink, pushes her arm through bottles of cleaning products, old sponges, old toothbrushes, toilet paper rolls and other junk to the shut-off valves.

ADELE (CONT'D)
I can't turn it! It's gonna flood!

Olive hugs the owl tightly and it speaks.

OWL
Whooo. Whooo. Whooo are you?

ADELE
I can't -- Oh wait, got it!

Adele turns off the water. Olive looks back into the room.

OLIVE
Mommy, Daddy has blood.

INT. EXAMINATION ROOM - WINTER 2005 - NIGHT

Caden sits on a metal table. The room has some meager Christmas ornaments. A doctor stitches Caden's forehead.

(CONTINUED)

Caden squints into the bright light the doctor uses to see his work. In the background we hear another patient.

                  PATIENT (O.S.)
         (crying)
   Please, please, please...

Caden sees a nurse shoving a tube far up into a man's nose. Another nurse wipes away the blood leaking out his nostril.

                  CADEN
   Will there be a scar?

                  DOCTOR
   Probably. It looks like a mudflap.

                  CADEN
   I prefer there not be a scar.

                  DOCTOR
   That fellow is annoying. He's in
   here every week. Like clockwork.

The off-screen patient continues to whimper. The doctor finishes his work on Caden.

                  DOCTOR (CONT'D)
   There. I think that should --

He looks at Caden's eyes, turns off the bright lamp and looks again. He turns the lamp back on and looks once more.

                  CADEN
   What?

The doctor feels Caden's pulse, then listens to his heart. He presses hard against the glands in Caden's neck.

                  DOCTOR
   Changes in bowel movements?

                  CADEN
   A little more yellow than usual.
   What?

                  DOCTOR
   I'd like you to see an
   ophthalmologist.

                  CADEN
   A neurologist?

9   CONTINUED: (2)

                    DOCTOR
          What? No, an ophthalmologist. I
          said, ophthalmologist.

                    CADEN
          Oh.

The doctor stares blankly at Caden for a long moment, then looks suspiciously in Caden's ears.

10 INT. CADEN AND ADELE'S CAR - WINTER 2006 - NIGHT

Adele drives and coughs spasmodically. The car swerves a bit. Caden has a bandaged head and a prescription in his hand. Olive, in her car seat, sings. Caden sees revelers in winter coats and party hats outside a house. They blow noisemakers and yell "happy new year!"

                    OLIVE
               (singing)
          It's a beautiful day and the sun is
          shining and yellow. And the world
          is too big to understand and today
          is Tuesday and --
               (speaking)
          Mom, is today Tuesday?

                    ADELE
          No, it's Friday, honey.

                    OLIVE
               (singing)
          And today is Friday and...

Olive's singing continues but goes under.

                    ADELE
          So what exactly did he say?

                    CADEN
          My pupils weren't properly dilating
          and, um, not doing the opposite ...

                    ADELE
          Constricting.

          CADEN   ADELE
No.   Yes. The bump to the head?

(CONTINUED)

CADEN
He doesn't know. Maybe. He said he doesn't think so. But maybe. But he doesn't know. But --

ADELE
Okay. I got it. Jesus.

CADEN
Sorry. I'm a little anxious.

OLIVE
Did you have to get a shot, Daddy?

CADEN
No, honey.
(to Adele)
It's the start of something awful.

OLIVE
Do I have to get a shot?

CADEN
What? No. Of course not.
(pause, to Adele)
This is really fucked timing.

ADELE
Caden.

CADEN
Sorry. Bad timing.

OLIVE
Did you tell him I have green poop?

ADELE (CONT'D)
Remind me to call the plumber, would you? I need a to-do list. Caden!

CADEN
(realizing)
I have rehearsal! Fuck!

CADEN
Sorry.

OLIVE
How many years till I have to get more shots?

ADELE (CONT'D)
Not for a long time, honey.

Caden pulls out a cell phone and dials.

OLIVE
A million years?

ADELE
Remember Dr. Woodman said after the last vaccination --

OLIVE
Dad, what's a plumber?

(CONTINUED)

CADEN
He's the man who --

ADELE
Or woman, Dad.

CADEN
Right. He's the man or woman who fixes sinks and toilets and... do you know what pipes are?

OLIVE
No.

CADEN
(into phone)
Hey, Jim. I know. I'm sorry. I had an accident. No, I'm okay.

OLIVE
Like to smoke out of?

CADEN
Different kind of pipe.
(into phone)
Just run lines. I'll be there soon. 'kay.
(hangs up)
Houses have pipes. They're, like, tubes and they're behind walls and under the floor everywhere and --

Olive begins to whimper in horror.

ADELE
What's wrong, baby?

OLIVE
(hushed anxious whisper)
Every-single-where?

CADEN
It's okay. They just carry water to and from sinks and bathtubs and toilets. It's like in your body you have veins and ... um...

ADELE
Capillaries.

CADEN
And they're filled with blood.

Olive is crying in earnest now.

(CONTINUED)

10 CONTINUED: (3)   10

                    OLIVE
          I don't want blood. I have blood?

                    ADELE
               (to Caden)
          What are you doing? Jesus.

                    CADEN
          I'm trying to explain plumbing.

                    ADELE
          Well, stop it.
               (to Olive)
          It's okay, honey.

                    OLIVE
               (weeping)
          I don't want blood. Will it hurt?
          Will it hurt, Daddy?!

                    CADEN
          No, honey, you're fine.

          OLIVE   CADEN
I don't want blood! I don't   (holding head)
want blood! I don't want   I can't do this now.
blood...

                    ADELE
          You don't have to worry, baby. You
          don't have blood.

                    CADEN
          Well, I don't think you should tell
          her she doesn't have blood.

                    ADELE
          Caden, stop it!

Olive cries. Adele coughs. Caden stares out the window. It's dark, but his pupils are pinpricks.

11 INT. OPHTHALMOLOGIST'S OFFICE - WINTER 2006 - DAY   11

An ophthalmologist examines Caden's eyes. An eyeglass calendar on the wall is open to March 2006.

                    CADEN
          Thanks for getting me in right
          away.

The doctor touches Caden's eye repeatedly with a small probe.

(CONTINUED)

CADEN (CONT'D)
Is it the bump to the head?

OPHTHALMOLOGIST
No.
     (writes in chart, then:)
Could be. But I think we need to
get you to a neurologist. Nothing
urgent.

CADEN
A neurologist?

OPHTHALMOLOGIST
Yes, a brain expert.

CADEN
I know what a neurologist is.

OPHTHALMOLOGIST
Fine. I just thought from
the way you asked --

CADEN
I thought maybe you said urologist.
Why do I need to see a neurologist?

OPHTHALMOLOGIST
For a look-see. The eyes are part
of the brain, after all.

CADEN
That's not true, is it?

OPHTHALMOLOGIST
Why would I say it if it weren't
true?

CADEN
It just doesn't seem right.

OPHTHALMOLOGIST
Like morally correct? Or right as
in accurate?

CADEN
I'm not sure. Accurate, I guess.

OPHTHALMOLOGIST
Hmm. Interesting.

The doctor writes in Caden's chart.

12 INT. SCHENECTADY THEATER - 2006 - DAY   12

Caden sits in the almost empty theater. A few people with
note-pads are scattered around. Centerstage, a 1948 Dodge
Business Coupe. The car is surrounded by various rooms from
that period: a kitchen, bedrooms, etc. Tom, the actor playing
Willy Loman, stands center stage. Claire, the actress playing
Linda Loman, sits in the set's bedroom. Davis, the actor
playing Biff, lies on the top bunk of a bunk bed upstage. A
fourth actor, playing Happy, lies on the bottom bunk.

                    CLAIRE (AS LINDA)
          Willy, you coming up!!!!

                    TOM (AS WILLY)
          Sssssh!!

                    CLAIRE (AS LINDA)
          Willy?

Tom climbs in the car.

                    CLAIRE (AS LINDA) (CONT'D)
          Willy? Answer me!...Willy!

Tom starts the car and guns the engine. A brick wall off
stage speeds into the car, accompanied by crashing and
screeching sound effects.

                    CLAIRE (AS LINDA) (CONT'D)
          No!!!

                    DAVIS (AS BIFF)
          Pop!!

The wall continues to be pulled past the car crashing into
the rest of the set, knocking walls over, creating havoc.

          CADEN   DAVID
Ok, ok, stop! David, what's   (looking back from seat)
happening here?   Sorry, Caden. Hold on.

David runs on stage to deal with the mess.

          DAVID (CONT'D)   CADEN
Andy? What just happened?   It's too late in the game to
                               be having these problems,
                               David.

          ANDY   DAVID
  (running in from wings)   I know, Caden. I'm sorry.
Shit. I don't know.   We'll get it. Andy?

                                              (CONTINUED)

Tom emerges from the car, covered with stage blood.

                    CADEN
          Please.
              (to Tom)
          That was good, Tom.

                    TOM
          Yeah? I was trying something
          different. I was crashing
          differently. Ambivalently.

                    CADEN
          I saw that. I like it.

Caden meets Tom at the foot of the stage. Behind them a group of technicians are lifting the wall and trying to re-set it. Claire primps in the bureau mirror.

                    CADEN (CONT'D)
          Try thinking of killing yourself as
          finally existing by ceasing to
          exist.

                    TOM
          Death is the only state in which
          Willy can contribute to the
          material plane?

                    CADEN
          Yes. Let's try it and see.
              (calling)
          How long, David?

                    DAVID
          I think fifteen. Andy?

          ANDY   CADEN
     Fifteen tops.   Why don't you get cleaned up,
                                Tom, and we'll go again.

Tom exits. Caden rubs his temples, then heads to the back of the house, pulling out his cell phone. He exits the theater.

INT. SCHENECTADY THEATER LOBBY - 2006 - DAY

Caden passes the box office. Hazel, 35, sits inside, reading a novel. She looks up, smiles warmly, and waves.

                    HAZEL
          I just heard the death of the
          salesman.

13   CONTINUED: 13

                         CADEN
               In more ways than one.

                         HAZEL
                    (compassionately)
               Oh no.
                    (then:)

                         CADEN
                    (holding up cell phone)
               In search of elusive signal.

                         HAZEL
               Signal's good here, oddly.

     She pats her lap in a friendly manner.

                         CADEN
               That is odd.

                         HAZEL
               I know! Cell phones, they're
               crazy!

               CADEN   HAZEL
          (chuckles)   (back in her book)
     See you in a few.   Yup.

14   EXT. SCHENECTADY THEATER - 2006 - DAY   14

     Caden has the phone to his ear. He's squinting in the bright
     sunlight, pupils dilated. The gaunt man watches him unseen.

                         CADEN
               Dr. Heshborg said I should see Dr.
               Scariano. My pupils don't work.

15   INT. SCHENECTADY THEATER BOX OFFICE - 2006 - CONTINUOUS   15

     Hazel reads the first page of <u>Swann's Way</u>. The other volumes
     of <u>In Search of Lost Time</u> are stacked neatly nearby. She
     looks up and sees Caden standing outside the box office
     window watching her.

                         HAZEL
               I keep reading the first line.
               It's a good line, I think. But I
               don't know much about literature.

                         CADEN
               Maybe you should read the first
               line of another series of books.

                                                          (CONTINUED)

CONTINUED:

HAZEL
I'm trying to better myself, Caden. Recommend me something. You're a genius; you must've read nearly a dozen books.

CADEN
Exactly twelve. Have you read Kafka?

HAZEL
Um, I've read his name. A lot! I swear!

CADEN
His whole name?

HAZEL
Okay, not his entire name. Heinz?

CADEN
(laughs)
You should read The Trial, maybe.

HAZEL
If you say so, I will. Can't wait till Wednesday. I'm so excited to see it.

CADEN
I hope you like it.

HAZEL
It's pretty impossible that I won't, you know. I mean...

She trails off, shrugs. They smile at each other. Caden exits. Hazel looks at her book, re-reads the first sentence.

INT. CADEN AND ADELE'S BATHROOM - 2006 - NIGHT

Caden sits on the toilet. He finishes, looks in the bowl. His bowel movement is dark and loose.

INT. CADEN AND ADELE'S BEDROOM - 2006 - NIGHT

Adele lies in bed asleep. Caden steps out of the bathroom and climbs into bed.

CADEN
I think I have blood in my stool.

(CONTINUED)

17   CONTINUED:

Adele looks over, half asleep.

              ADELE
     That stool in your office?

18   INT. THERAPIST'S OFFICE - 2006 - DAY

Caden and Adele sit across from Madeline, 40's, their therapist. Silence. Adele has a coughing fit. Then:

              ADELE
     When I was pregnant with Olive...

             MADELINE
     What was it like?

              ADELE
     Um... I don't know. Hopeful or
     something. Like something was
     going to change.

             MADELINE
     Something did, no?

    ADELE   CADEN
Yes, of course.   Yes. I mean... big time.

              ADELE
     Maybe not as much as I had hoped.
     That's a terrible thing to say.

             MADELINE
     There are no terrible things to say
     in here. Only true and false.

              ADELE
     I feel alone sometimes. I feel
     exhausted. Can I say something
     awful?

             MADELINE
     Yes. Please do.

              ADELE
     I've fantasized about Caden dying
     and being able to start again.
     Guilt free. I know it's terrible.

19 EXT. SCHENECTADY THEATER - 2006 - DAY   19

Caden sits sadly on the steps; drinks coffee. He watches as Hazel pulls into the parking lot, gets out of her car. The gaunt man is behind the trash bin. She sits next to Caden.

                  CADEN
It's a nightmare in there.

                  HAZEL
The car crash?

                  CADEN
Well... not only.

                  HAZEL
Sorry. So I'm reading <u>The Trial</u>.

                  CADEN
Yeah? You like?

                  HAZEL
Love. I'm such an idiot for not knowing about this book.
       (conspiratorial whisper)
It's famous, it turns out.

                  CADEN
You're not an idiot.

Pause.

                  HAZEL
Then you say, in fact, you're very bright, Hazel. And I love your eyes.

      CADEN   HAZEL
In fact, you're very bright,   (playing charmed)
Hazel. And I love your eyes.   Oh, *am* I? Oh, *do* you? Oh, darling!

                  CADEN
Then what do I say?

                  HAZEL
I can't say what then you say.

                  CADEN
Why?

(CONTINUED)

                    HAZEL
            Cause it's dirty.

A whistling noise turns their heads. In the distance a man
with an unopened parachute is plummeting.

                    HAZEL (CONT'D)
            Oh my God! Jesus!

They watch as the man falls behind a building. A scream. A
screech of brakes.

                    HAZEL (CONT'D)
            He's gotta be dead. Right?

INT. CADEN AND ADELE'S BATHROOM - 2006 - DAY

Caden enters. The plumber is working on the sink.

                    PLUMBER
            Go ahead. I've seen boy parts.

INT. ADELE'S STUDIO - 2006 - DAY

The studio is a mess, the floor covered with paint. Adele,
in her paint-spattered clothing, works on a tiny canvas, an
inch square. She paints with a single-hair brush while
looking through a magnifying glass. Caden pokes his head in.

                    CADEN
            Can I piss in your sink?

                    ADELE
            Um, yeah, I guess.

Caden pisses in the sink in the corner of the studio. His
urine is amber. He finishes and peeks over Adele's shoulder,
through the magnifying glass at the painting. It's an
amazingly detailed and angrily colored painting of a woman in
a state of profound despair, screaming to the heavens, while
standing in a field of flames.

                    CADEN
            It's gorgeous, Ad.

                    ADELE
            Thanks. How was rehearsal?

                    CADEN
            Awful. We have five hundred and
            sixty lighting cues. I don't know
            why I made it so complicated.

                                                    (CONTINUED)

CONTINUED:

ADELE
It's what you do.

CADEN
Yeah. Anyway, we got through it. I think you'll be impressed.

ADELE
Caden, listen, I'm really sorry. I just can't go tonight.
(off his look)
I'm sorry. I've got to get two canvases ready to ship. By tomorrow. I know it sucks.

CADEN
But it's opening night.

ADELE
I know. I'm sorry. I would go if I could.

CADEN
I have to get ready.

ADELE
I'll go tomorrow! We'll make tomorrow like the premiere!

CADEN
I mean, I can't take a dump in your sink! What am I supposed to do? I have to get ready!

INT. SCHENECTADY THEATER - 2006 - NIGHT

The theater is full. Caden stands nervously in the back. The lights dim. Hazel looks back from her seat at Caden and mouths the word "yay." He smiles. The curtain rises on a dark stage. Tom, as Willy, gets out of the car parked center stage and walks into the kitchen.

TOM (AS WILLY)
Oh boy, oh boy.

CLAIRE (AS LINDA)
Willy!

TOM (AS WILLY)
It's all right, I came back.

CLAIRE (AS LINDA)
Why? What happened?
(pause)
Did something happen, Willy?

TOM (AS WILLY)
No, nothing happened.

(CONTINUED)

CONTINUED:

> CLAIRE (AS LINDA)
> You didn't smash the car, did you?

> TOM (AS WILLY)
> I said nothing happened. Didn't you hear me?

> CLAIRE (AS LINDA)
> Don't you feel well?

> TOM (AS WILLY)
> I'm tired to death. I couldn't make it. I just couldn't make it, Linda.

> CLAIRE (AS LINDA)
> Where were you all day? You look terrible.

> TOM (AS WILLY)
> I got as far as a little above Yonkers. I stopped for a cup of coffee... maybe it was the coffee.

> CLAIRE (AS LINDA)
> What?

> TOM (AS WILLY)
> I suddenly couldn't drive any more. The car kept going off onto the shoulder, y'know?

The audience is rapt. Caden relaxes.

INT. QUINCY'S, BACK ROOM - 2006 - NIGHT

The cast party is in full swing. The opening was a success. Lots of drinking. Caden chats with Claire. Hazel watches from across the room.

> CLAIRE
> (scrunching her nose)
> Ugh, I hated myself tonight. Plus I'm so bloated and enormous.

CADEN	CLAIRE
No. You looked great. You were great. I was very pleased.	I thought Tom was amazing!

(CONTINUED)

CADEN
Yeah. Absolutely.
(squints suddenly)
Sorry. I have a bit of a headache.

CLAIRE
(kisses his forehead)
I just want to thank you for everything. You've been absolutely brilliant and it's going to be miserable going ahead without you.

CADEN
I'll be around. I'll check in.

She gets teary, gives him a kiss on the cheek.

CLAIRE
God, I'm such a baby.

She just looks at him and smiles and nods.

CLAIRE (CONT'D)
I'm going to get drunk, that's what.

CADEN
Ok, Claire.

She backs away and gets lost in the crowd. Caden massages his temples. Suddenly Hazel is next to him.

HAZEL
I figured I'd better get in fast.

CADEN
Hey!

HAZEL
I loved it! And, by the way, Claire is trouble. And not terribly bright.

Caden laughs.

HAZEL (CONT'D)
Just wanted you to know the word on the street.

CADEN
So you liked it?

(CONTINUED)

                    HAZEL
          Are you kidding? I cried for like
          fifteen minutes after. I loved
          every minute of it. Except Claire.
          I thought she was weak.

                    CADEN
          Easy on the eyes.

                    HAZEL
          Oh, Caden, not you, too.

He laughs. They sip their drinks.

                    HAZEL (CONT'D)
          Where's el wife-o?

                    CADEN
          Had to work. Her Berlin show is in
          two weeks. We're going to spend
          like a month there.

                    HAZEL
          Ah.

                    CADEN
          Ah.

                    HAZEL
          Ah.

                    CADEN
          Choo!

                    HAZEL
          Hooray! We've still got it!
              (pause)
          I'll miss you.

                    CADEN
          Yeah, me too.

          HAZEL   CADEN
You're going to miss you?   Yeah, that's it.

                    HAZEL
              (pause)
          Why do I like you so much?

                    CADEN
          I couldn't begin to guess.

                                              (CONTINUED)

HAZEL
(sighing)
Me neither. It must be that you're married. Do you get high, my friend?

CADEN
Y'know. Sometimes.

HAZEL
You want to now? With me. In my car.

CADEN
I don't know.

HAZEL
Come on, it's a party.

CADEN
I get kind of... *something* when I'm stoned.

HAZEL
What does *something* mean?

CADEN
I don't know. Bothered?

HAZEL
What does bothered mean?

CADEN
Y'know... *bothered*. Horny.

HAZEL
And me with a station wagon and all. Could be dangerous.

CADEN
(laughing)
Yeah, it really could.

HAZEL
You're absolutely zero fun.

CADEN
You know I wish I could.

HAZEL
Jesus, I like you. I'm going.

CADEN
You're not staying for the reviews?

(CONTINUED)

CONTINUED: (4)

> HAZEL
> I know it's brilliant. I don't need some dope with elbow patches telling me.

She smiles, gives him a hug, and heads toward the door.

INT. HAZEL'S CAR - 2006 - NIGHT

Hazel drives down a dark street, crying. People watch her passing car from various windows. There's a run-over dog, lit by a streetlight, glistening on the side of the road.

EXT. RESIDENTIAL SCHENECTADY STREET - 2006 - A FEW MOMENTS LATER

Hazel studies the dog. It's a bloody, gutty mess, squashed flat. Against all odds, it's still alive. Its head is lolling. She bends down to pet it.

> HAZEL
> You're not going to make it, baby.

INT. HAZEL'S BATHROOM (APARTMENT) - 2006 - NIGHT

Hazel takes off her make-up, hair back in a clip. She watches herself blankly in the mirror, somewhat erased without eye make-up. The run-over dog is sleeping in a box on the floor.

INT. QUINCY'S, BACK ROOM - 2006 - ABOUT DAWN

The party has thinned out. The remaining people are sitting around a table, drinking. Claire, next to Caden, rests her head, sleepily drunk, against his shoulder. Caden studies a series of lumps under the skin of his arm.

> CLAIRE
> What are you going to do now?

> CADEN
> I'm going to Berlin for a month for my wife's show. Then I don't know.

> CLAIRE
> I wish I was your wife or a wife or had a wife. Or was German even. I'm so lonely with none of those things.

A man walks in with a bunch of newspapers.

(CONTINUED)

CONTINUED:

                    CADEN
          Yay or nay?

EXT. BURNING HOUSE - 2006 - DAY

Hazel gets out of her car and walks up to a neat little house on a street of neat little houses. Faint swirls of smoke escape from the windows. She rings the doorbell. The button is hot; Hazel pulls her finger away.

INT. BURNING HOUSE - 2006 - A FEW MOMENTS LATER

The rooms are hazy. The realtor coughs a little. Hazel surveys the scene.

                    HAZEL
          I've always loved this house.

          REALTOR   HAZEL
Yes. It's a wonderful place.   The truth is, I never really
                                imagined I could afford it.

                    REALTOR
          The sellers are very motivated now.

                    HAZEL
          It's a scary decision. I never
          thought I'd buy a house alone.
          But, y'know, I'm 36, and I wonder
          what I'm really waiting for.

          REALTOR   HAZEL
Home-buying is always scary.   But I mean with the fire and
                                all especially.

                    REALTOR
          It's a good size though, twenty-two
          hundred square feet. Not including
          the partially-finished basement

          HAZEL   REALTOR
I don't know. I'm thinking I   It's a perfect size for
should go.   someone alone.

                    HAZEL
          I like it, I do. But I'm really
          concerned about dying in the fire.

                    REALTOR
          It's a big decision, how one
          prefers to die. Would you like to
          meet my son? Derek?

(CONTINUED)

29 CONTINUED: 29

Derek, 40 and scruffily handsome, appears around a corner.

          DEREK   REALTOR
Hey, Mom.   Derek's living in the
                              basement since his divorce.
                              If that's okay.

30 INT. ADELE AND CADEN'S LIVING ROOM - 2006 - DAWN   30

Caden enters. Adele sits at the table across from Maria, 40. They are drunk and eating nachos.

          ADELE   CADEN
Hey.   Hey.

                MARIA
        Hi, Caden. How'd it go?

                CADEN
        Hi. It's late.

                ADELE
        Maria came over to keep me company
        and we lost track. I'm sorry I
        missed the play. But I got
        everything done here. How'd it go?

                CADEN
        We're a hit. Reviews are great.   *
        New York Times said it was   *
        brilliant to cast young actors as   *
        Willy and Linda.   *

          ADELE   MARIA
Great.   That's great, Caden! Good
                              for you!

                ADELE
        I'll see it tomorrow. Tonight!

Adele and Maria laugh.

          MARIA   ADELE
Jesus, it is late. Early!   Can we get a ticket for
I'd love to see it, too.   Maria?

Adele smiles.

                CADEN
        Are you stoned?

(CONTINUED)

CONTINUED:

> **ADELE**
> A little. I don't know. Y'know? I mean, are you happy with it?

> **CADEN**
> Yeah. Love to know what you think.

> **ADELE**
> It doesn't matter what I think.

> **MARIA**
> Absolutely! It's all about your artistic satisfaction, Caden.

EXT. RESIDENTIAL SCHENECTADY STREET - SPRING 2006 - DAY

Caden and Olive walk along. Caden holds a tax envelope. His face has pustules on it. The gaunt man follows.

> **OLIVE**
> What's wrong with your face, Daddy?

> **CADEN**
> It's pustules. It's called sycosis. Spelled differently than psychosis, but it sounds the same.

> **OLIVE**
> I don't know what that means.

> **CADEN**
> Well, there's two different kinds of psychosis. They're spelled differently. P-s-y is like if you're crazy and s-y is like these things on my face.

> **OLIVE**
> You could have both though.

> **CADEN**
> I could. But I don't.

> **OLIVE**
> Okay, pretend we're fairies. I'm a girl fairy and my name is ... La-ru...lee. And you're a boy fairy and your name is Teeteree.

> **CADEN**
> Ok.

(CONTINUED)

31 CONTINUED:

>   OLIVE
>   What's my name again?
>
>   CADEN
>   La-ru-lee.
>
>   OLIVE
>   No. I said ... La-ru-la...ay.

32 INT. SCHENECTADY POST OFFICE - SPRING 2006 - CONTINUOUS

Caden and Olive are at the back of the long line of people.

>   OLIVE
>   Pretend we fight each other. And I
>   say stop hitting me or I'll die.
>   And you say okay, but you're
>   fibbing. And you hit me again.
>
>   CADEN
>   Okay.
>
>   OLIVE
>   Okay. Let's go. Hit me.

They pretend to hit each other. Olive makes hissing and roaring noises. She stops.

>   OLIVE (CONT'D)
>   Okay. You have to stop hitting me
>   now or I will die.
>
>   CADEN
>   Okay.

He stops.

>   OLIVE
>   No! Pretend you're fibbing!
>   Remember?

He mock hits her again. She falls.

>   OLIVE (CONT'D)
>   Now I have to die.
>   (beat)
>   Pretend you say you don't want me
>   to die.
>
>   CADEN
>   I don't want you to die.

(CONTINUED)

                    OLIVE
                (compassionate whisper)
            But I have to.

                    CADEN
            But I'll miss you.

                    OLIVE
            I have to. And you'll have to wait
            a million years to see me again.

Caden tears up at this and tries to conceal it.

                    OLIVE (CONT'D)
            And I'll be put in a box. And all
            I'll need is a tiny glass of water.
            And lots of -- tiny pieces of
            pizza. And the box will have
            wings, like an airplane.

                    CADEN
            Where will it take you?

                    OLIVE
                (thinks)
            Home.

33   INT. SCHENECTADY THEATER - SPRING 2006 - NIGHT

Performance in progress. There is now a cemetery on stage. Linda, Biff, and other characters stand around a gravesite. Caden sits in the audience between Adele and Maria and his parents. He glances over at Adele's stony face. Maria is drunk and blurry.

                    DAVIS (AS BIFF)
            Let's go, Mom.

                    CLAIRE (AS LINDA)
            I'll be with you in a minute. Go
            on, Charley. I want to, just a
            minute.

The other characters exit the stage.

                    CLAIRE (AS LINDA) (CONT'D)
                (talking to the grave)
            I never had a chance to say good-
            bye. Forgive me, dear. I can't cry.
            I don't understand it; I can't cry.
            It seems to me that you're just on
            another trip. I keep expecting you.
                    (MORE)

(CONTINUED)

CONTINUED:

> **CLAIRE (AS LINDA) (CONT'D)**
> Willy, dear, why did you do it? I search and search and I search, and I can't understand it, Willy. I made the last payment on the house today. Today, dear. And there'll be nobody home. We're free and clear… We're free… We're free… We're free…

The stage lights go dark.

EXT. URBAN-ISH SCHENECTADY STREET - SPRING 2006 - NIGHT

Caden, Adele, Maria, and his parents walk along.

CADEN	ADELE
I just --	I don't know what it matters what I think.

> **CADEN'S MOTHER**
> I loved the story. So interesting.

CADEN	ADELE
Because your opinion is --	It was good. It was well done. It was very ... successful.

> **MARIA**
> Oh, I thought it was wonnnderful!

> **CADEN'S FATHER**
> Why were the old people so young?

CADEN	ADELE
It was a choice, Dad. I'll explain later. (to Adele) But?	Nothing. But nothing. (pause) I can't get excited about your restaging someone else's old play. There's nothing personal in it.

CADEN	CADEN'S FATHER
I put my soul into that thing.	I mean, they were younger than their kids. That doesn't make sense.

> **ADELE**
> Do you really believe that tripe?

CADEN	CADEN'S MOTHER
Wow. It's not tripe. Jesus.	I liked that the old people were so young. It was interesting.

(CONTINUED)

CONTINUED:

ADELE (CONT'D)
Ok, fine. But it's not you. It's not anyone. It's not real.

CADEN
People come out crying, saying their lives are changed and --

ADELE
Great. Be a fucking tool of suburban blue-hair regional theater subscribers. But what are you leaving behind? You act as if you have forever to figure it out.

CADEN
Why are you being like this?

Adele has a coughing fit.

ADELE
I'm not being like anything.

CADEN
Are you seeing someone else?

ADELE
Is that your entire frame of reference for relationship problems?

CADEN
No. I don't know. It's a stressful time. Our shows. The whole health thing.

ADELE
Oh, you're fine.

INT. CADEN AND ADELE'S LIVING ROOM - SPRING 2006 - MORNING

Caden, in shorts and t-shirt, tiptoes past his parents, sleeping on the fold-out couch.

INT. CADEN AND ADELE'S KITCHEN - SPRING 2006 - MORNING

Adele sits at the kitchen table with Olive. She drinks coffee and talks on the phone. Olive eats cereal and watches a cartoon. Caden enters. Olive doesn't look away from her show. A cartoon jackal talks to a man who looks like Caden.

JACKAL
When you are dead there is no time. The world is a timeless rock.

Caden pours a cup of coffee, sits down at the table.

(CONTINUED)

CONTINUED:

> CADEN
> I think I might have arthritis.

Adele continues to talk on the phone.

> ADELE
> No, I know. Exactly.

Caden picks up the newspaper. It's dated May 25th, 2006. He flips through, finds the obituaries and starts to read.

> ADELE (CONT'D)
> Ok. All right. Yeah. Ok, bye.

Adele hangs up the phone, looks at the paper.

> CADEN
> My joints are stiff. Who was that?

> ADELE
> Maria.

> CADEN
> Right. It's been three hours since you spoke.

> ADELE
> Caden, I think I want to go to Berlin with just Olive.

Caden looks up.

> ADELE (CONT'D)
> I think it would be good for us.

Silence. Caden's father appears in the doorway.

> CADEN'S FATHER
> Morning, kiddos.

> CADEN
> (to Adele)
> Christ. Is this about last night?

Caden's father smiles, nods, and exits.

INT. CADEN AND ADELE'S BEDROOM - SPRING 2006 - NIGHT

Adele packs. Caden sits on the bed.

> CADEN
> Can I ask you a question, Ad?

She looks up at him.

(CONTINUED)

CONTINUED:

CADEN (CONT'D)
Have I disappointed you somehow?

She starts to cry, hugs him.

ADELE
Caden. I don't know. Y'know? I don't know what I'm doing. It's just a little time apart.
(pause)
We'll talk when I get back. Everyone is disappointing. The more you know someone. The whole romantic love thing is just projection. Right? I don't know.
(pause)
I'm sorry. I love you. I don't know what I'm doing. We'll talk when I get back.

38 INT. ADELE'S STUDIO - 2006 - DAY

Cobwebs. The room is long abandoned. Caden slumps against a wall and stares into space. He starts to cry and can't stop.

Later: Caden watches a paint-spattered TV. A commercial: diffused images of people flying kites, having picnics, watching sunsets. A shot of Caden among them.

ANNOUNCER
Flurostatin TR allows you to live life when it's your turn to face the challenges of chemotherapy. Ask your doctor if it's right for you.

He feels the bumps on his arm, which have grown. He writes down Fluorostatin TR. He starts to clean Adele's studio.

Later: The room is sparkling. No more paint anywhere. Caden is on his knees, scrubbing the last bit of dirt. He is sweaty and focused.

39 INT. SCHENECTADY THEATER BOX OFFICE - 2006 - DAY

Caden, neatly groomed, leans on the counter chatting with Hazel. Her crushed dog sleeps on the floor in a box.

HAZEL
We should get a drink. Be fun.

(CONTINUED)

CONTINUED:

> CADEN
> Be weird.

> HAZEL
> I like weird. I like *you*. See?

He doesn't say anything.

> HAZEL (CONT'D)
> Anyway. I don't want to make you uncomfortable. I just thought it would be a fun diversion. Okay, I do want to make you uncomfortable.

> CADEN
> (laughs)
> Oh, Haze. I wish I could.

> HAZEL
> You can, *Cade*. You can!

> CADEN
> I have an appointment.

> HAZEL
> Crease.

> CADEN
> What do you mean?

> HAZEL
> It's just a word. Don't get all bent out of shape. Jeez.

> CADEN
> I won't. Sorry.

INT. DENTIST'S OFFICE - 2006 - DAY

The masked dentist probes Caden's mouth.

> DENTIST
> 3, 3, 3. 3, 3, 5. 3, 4, 3. 3, 4, 4. 5, 3, 3. 2, 4, 3.
> (to Caden)
> Some fives this time. Not good. Keep with the flossing. We'll see in three months.

INT. THERAPIST'S OFFICE - DAY

Caden sits across from Madeline.

(CONTINUED)

41   CONTINUED: 41

                CADEN   MADELINE
         I'm lonely.   Yes. Anything else?

    Caden notices Madeline's feet in too-small shoes. There are
    visible blisters and band-aids on her feet.

                CADEN   MADELINE
         I'm hurt.   Yes. And?

                CADEN   MADELINE
         I think Adele's right when   What would be real?
         she says I'm not doing
         anything real.

                         CADEN
                  I'm afraid I'm going to die. They
                  don't know what's wrong with me. I
                  want to do something important.
                  While I'm still here.

                         MADELINE
                  That would be the time to do it,
                  yes. I have a book that might help
                  you get better.

                CADEN   MADELINE
         Better?   Yes. It's called Getting
                                            Better.

                         CADEN
                  Who wrote it?

                MADELINE   CADEN
         I did.   Oh.
           (goes to full bookcase)   (looking at titles)
         All of these.   Wow. I never knew that.

                         MADELINE
                  Wow. Yes, wow. Wow indeed.

    She hands Caden the very thick book. He flips through it,
    catching words and snippets here and there: *Clairaudience
    ... vaginal juices... The echo began ... Plumbing ... Cats
    eat rats ... Me who am as a raw nerve ... Crease.*

                         MADELINE (CONT'D)
                  That's forty-five dollars. Wow.

42   INT. CADEN'S OFFICE - 2006 - NIGHT   42

    Caden finds a website online for Madeline Gravis. Amazing
    graphics.

                                                            (CONTINUED)

42   CONTINUED: 42

She is touted as one of the foremost psychologists in the world, a sought-after public speaker, advisor to world leaders. Her book <u>Getting Better</u> has sold millions of copies and is translated into fifteen languages. In a box at the bottom is a photo of a smiling Caden; it reads: Theater Director Caden Cotard says, "It'll change my life!"

43   INT. DENTIST'S OFFICE - 2006 - DAY   43

The dentist probes Caden's mouth. The Hygienist writes the numbers.

                    DENTIST
          5, 6, 5. 5, 5, 6. 4, 6, 5.
              (to Caden)
          I'm going to recommend a
          periodontist. He'll probably
          recommend gum surgery.

44   INT. CADEN AND ADELE'S LIVING ROOM - 2006 - DAY   44

Caden is on the phone. His legs are elevated and his pant legs are rolled up, revealing swollen, discolored calves.

                    CADEN
          I'm looking for... I'm sorry, I
          don't speak German. No. I'm --

45   INT. QUINCY'S - 2007 - NIGHT   45

Caden sits by himself in a booth, reading the self-help book.

                    VOICE
          We must live in the present moment.
          The now. The now. The now.

Caden tries to be in the present moment as a women sings about cancer on a small stage in the back.

Later: Caden nurses a beer. He seems unwell. Hazel plops down across from him. She has a smudge of soot on her nose.

                    CADEN
          Hey! Thanks for meeting me.

He points to his nose. She wipes at the soot on hers.

                    HAZEL
          God, I'm delighted. Thought you'd
          never ask. You did ask, right?

                    CADEN
          I didn't want to be alone.

                                                        (CONTINUED)

HAZEL
Who does?
(pause)
You don't look like you feel well.

CADEN
I'm going through some things.

HAZEL
You want to tell me about it?

CADEN
I can't really. But I'm meditating and running and taking vitamins. Cutting out sugar. I can't really say any more. It's...

HAZEL
Ok. Tell me something else.

CADEN
You tell me something. Oh. I've cut out wheat.

HAZEL
Um, I bought this really nifty sweater today. On sale. Fifty dollars reduced from three hundred!

CADEN
It's beautiful.

HAZEL
It's cashmere. So very soft. You must feel it.

Hazel holds her arm out. Caden touches it.

CADEN
What do we do with all this, Hazel?

HAZEL
I don't know. We fuck? We continue to sort of flirt? You divorce your wife and marry me and I make you happy for the very first time in your life and all your symptoms disappear?
(beat)
We call it a day?
(beat)
Don't choose the last one. I just said that one for effect.

(CONTINUED)

CONTINUED: (2)

CADEN
Do I have to choose at all?

HAZEL
No, I suppose not. Choosing is not your strong suit. You want to come over to my place, Cotard?

CADEN
Um ...

HAZEL
I'm won't let you off the hook by saying "never mind" this time.

CADEN
Adele is only on vacation.

HAZEL
She hasn't called you since she left. You've left countless messages. It's been a year.

CADEN
It's been a week.

HAZEL
(stares at him, then:)
I'm going to buy you a calendar.

Caden rips a cocktail napkin into little pieces.

CADEN
Okay, just for one drink.

Hazel smiles and stands. She scoops up the torn napkin pieces and puts them in her purse.

HAZEL
Scraps for my scrapbook.

Caden watches her ass as she turns to leave.

INT. HAZEL'S CAR - 2007 - NIGHT

Hazel drives. Caden follows in his car. We see him in her rearview mirror, peering into her car. Hazel hikes her skirt and causally begins to play with herself with her right hand.

INT. BURNING HOUSE - KITCHEN - 2007 - NIGHT

Hazel fixes drinks, mixes them with her right index finger. She hands Caden one.

(CONTINUED)

CADEN
I really can't drink very much because of my condition.

HAZEL
Caden's mysterious condition. Well, have one sip, anyway.

CADEN
Did you put something in it?

HAZEL
Would you like me to have? A little love potion, perhaps?

CADEN
Sure, why not?

HAZEL
If that's what it takes, consider it done. Poof! Love potion number 69.

Caden laughs and takes a sip.

CADEN
It's good.

She takes a sip of her drink. Caden drinks some more of his.

HAZEL
Does it make you want to kiss me?

CADEN
Yeah. Kind of.

HAZEL
Tell me why?

CADEN
Um, I feel a lot of longing.

HAZEL
Hmm. Beg a girl, why dontcha.

CADEN	HAZEL
Um, okay. Please, Hazel, let me --	On your knees.

CADEN
What?

                        HAZEL
            I'd like you to beg me on your
            knees for a kiss. Just for fun.

Dumbly, Caden gets down on his knees.

                        CADEN
            Why am I doing this?

                        HAZEL
                (smiling warmly)
            For fun, baby.

                        CADEN
            You'll help me forget my troubles?

                        HAZEL
            Oh, kiddo, you don't even know.

                        CADEN
            I have a wife.

                        HAZEL
            You have me. And I adore you.

INT. BURNING HOUSE - BEDROOM - 2007 - NIGHT

Caden and Hazel have violent sex. Hazel watches Caden's
contorted face. They finish and lie there. Caden starts to
weep.

                        HAZEL
            What? What is it?

            CADEN   HAZEL
I don't know. I'm sorry.   What?

                        CADEN
            I'm just so confused. I'm sorry.
            I'm really sick. I think I'm
            dying. I have a kid. I'm married.

            HAZEL   CADEN
Oh, Jesus. Oh, fuck *me*.   I'm sorry. It's terrible, I
                                know.

                        HAZEL
            Yeah. I just thought this might
            change things. I hoped. Ugh.

(CONTINUED)

48   CONTINUED: 48

                    CADEN
               (still crying)
          I had a good time. I think you're
          a very nice person. Really.

                    HAZEL
          That is just the wrong thing to say
          right now, Caden. You should go.

49   INT. CADEN AND ADELE'S LIVING ROOM - 2008 - NIGHT   49

     Caden is on the phone.

                    CADEN
               (crying)
          I'm so glad I finally got you.

                                        INTERCUT WITH:

A50 INT. ADELE'S BERLIN APARTMENT - 2008 - SAME   A50

     Adele stands at the far end of her apartment, near a window.
     She shouts into the phone.

                    ADELE
          Hello? Hello? Who is this?

                    CADEN
          It's Caden!

                    ADELE
          Ellen?

                    CADEN
          Caden! I can't wait to see you and
          Olive on the 12th. um... I went
          someplace without you tonight, Ad.
          I went some place you couldn't come
          with me. I'm sorry.

                    ADELE
          What? Who is this? Oh, I have to
          go. There's a party. I'm famous!

                    CADEN
          Oh. Ok. Great. Have fu --

     The connection is lost. Caden sits there, looks at the 2007
     tax form in front of him, goes into convulsions. He manages
     to grab the phone, his hand flopping all over the dial.

                                                    (CONTINUED)

A50   CONTINUED: A50

> OPERATOR
> 911. What's the problem, ma'am?

> CADEN
> I'm sick.

> OPERATOR
> We're out of ambulances, miss, but we'll send a taxi. Please wait in front of your house, miss.

50   INT. CAB - 2008 - NIGHT   50

Caden sits crammed in the back of a cab with three other sick people. The guy next to Caden is bleeding profusely from his nose, and holds a handful of balled-up tissues to his face.

> DRIVER
> (studying Caden in mirror)
> You were supposed to be a woman.

> CADEN
> How do you mean?

> DRIVER
> Well, no matter. I get almost the same money either way.

Blood drips out of the man's nose onto Caden's shoulder. The cab pulls into a loading dock area.

A51   EXT. HOSPITAL LOADING DOCK - 2008 - CONTINUOUS   A51

There are filthy dumpsters back here, piled high with used bandages.

> DRIVER
> (pointing to door)
> Go through there. Don't touch any garbage. Especially those of you with open wounds.

> NOSE MAN
> I have an open nose wound.

> CADEN
> I think I'll just go home. I'm feeling better.

> DRIVER
> You have to register. You called 911. You're on record.
> (MORE)

(CONTINUED)

A51 CONTINUED: A51

                    DRIVER (CONT'D)
               If you don't go in, I get fined.
               And I'll fucking hunt you down and
               kill you.

51   INT. HOSPITAL - 2008 - NIGHT   51

     Caden waits on a plastic chair in a dimly lit hallway, his
     beat-up suitcase at his feet. He reads a very old Vogue and
     opens to a spread about his wife. She seems glamorous.
     There are photos of her in Berlin, her work, her flat. She is
     the toast of the art world. Photos of her with two men, and
     also with Olive, who seems somewhat Nazi Youth-like now.

                    NURSE
               Mr. Cotard?

     He looks up, having forgotten where he was. He grabs his
     suitcase and follows the nurse down a dismal hallway: gurneys
     against dirty walls, empty wheelchairs. Skinny man takes a
     flash picture of Caden. Nurses drinking coffee out of paper
     cups eye him. Puddles of vomit on the floor. They arrive at
     the end of the hall. A doctor pokes his head out of a room.
     He studies a file and doesn't look up.

                    DOCTOR
               Mr. Cotard?

52   INT. SMALL EXAMINING ROOM - 2008 - CONTINUOUS   52

     The doctor never looks up from the files.

                    DOCTOR
               You've had a seizure of sorts.

          CADEN   DOCTOR
     What does that mean?   Seems to be some synaptic
                                     degradation. Fungal in
                                     origin. Autonomic functions
                                     going haywire.

                    CADEN
               It's serious?

                    DOCTOR
               We don't know but yes.

     They both sit there in silence for a long while.

                    DOCTOR (CONT'D)
               We'll get you enrolled a
               biofeedback program. Maybe you can
               learn some sort of manual override.

53 INT. SCHENECTADY POST OFFICE - WINTER 2008 - DAY 53

Caden waits in line, holding a big wrapped box, addressed to Olive in Germany.

54 INT. CADEN AND ADELE'S LIVING ROOM - WINTER 2008 - NIGHT 54

Caden sits on the couch, wheezing and reading a dictionary entry for the word "crease." The definition is "n. a fold." He squirts artificial saliva in his mouth.

55 OMITTED 55

56 INT. PERIODONTIST'S OFFICE - WINTER 2008 - DAY 56

Caden is having periodontal surgery. It's bloody.

57 INT. SCHENECTADY THEATER LOBBY - WINTER 2008 - NIGHT 57

Caden, with swollen lower face and bleeding mouth, approaches the box office with a gift-wrapped box. Hazel looks up. The damaged dog barks.

          HAZEL   CADEN
Be quiet, Squishy.   Hi.

          HAZEL
Caden, I won't be yet another woman you feel guilty about.

          CADEN
Okay. Thank you anyway.

          HAZEL
Here. Take this. I got like five for Christmas. Goddamn Christmas.

She hands him a 2009 calendar. It features photos of Adele.

58 INT. CADEN'S OFFICE - SPRING 2009 - NIGHT 58

Adele calender on wall, open to March. Caden reads <u>Getting Better</u>:

          VOICE
Now. Now. Now! Be here now!

                        INTERCUT WITH:

A59 INT. ADELE'S BERLIN APARTMENT - 2009 - SAME A59

Adele feeds a piece of paper into a fax machine.

                                  (CONTINUED)

A59   CONTINUED: A59

A fax starts to come in. Caden watches as the words appear, fuzzy as if there is some interference in the process.

Olive wanted me to ask you <u>not</u> to read her diary. She left it under her pillow by mistake. Glglf n mesr-siy. Hewz wec.

59   INT. OLIVE'S ROOM - 2009 - NIGHT   59

Caden lifts the bed pillow and finds a kid's diary. He studies it, puts it back. There's a knock at the front door.

60   INT. CADEN AND ADELE'S LIVING ROOM - 2009 - NIGHT   60

Caden opens the front door. A man hands him an envelope.

61   INT. THERAPIST'S OFFICE - 2009 - DAY   61

Madeline's feet are swollen and bloody.

          CADEN   MADELINE
So I just got this MacArthur   Oh, Caden!
Grant last night.

          CADEN   MADELINE
Yeah. A lot of money.   Do you know what you're going
                                      to do with it?

                    CADEN
       A theater piece. Something big and
       true and tough. Y'know, finally
       put my real self into something.

         MADELINE   CADEN
Oh, Caden! What is your real   I don't know yet. The
self, do you think?   MacArthur is called "the
                                      genius grant." And I want to
                                      earn it.

                  MADELINE
       That's wonderful. God bless! I
       guess you'll have to discover your
       real self. Right?

                    CADEN
       Yeah, I mean, yeah. Oh, I wanted
       to ask you, how old are kids when
       they start to write?

                  MADELINE
       Varies.

(CONTINUED)

CADEN
Could a four year old keep a diary?

MADELINE
Listen, there's an absolutely brilliant novel written by a four year old.

CADEN
Really?

MADELINE
Little Winky. By Horace Azpiazu.

CADEN
Aww. Cute.

MADELINE
Hardly. Little Winky is a virulent anti-Semite. The story follows his initiation into the Klan, his immersion in the pornographic snuff industry and his ultimate degradation at the hands of a black ex-convict named Eric Washington Jackson Jones... Johnson... Jefferson, with whom he embarks on a brutal homosexual affair.

CADEN
Wow. Written by a four year old?

MADELINE
Azpiazu killed himself at five.

CADEN
That's horrible.

MADELINE
He would've written so much more had he lived. They developed a method -- some software -- to determine what he would've written had he lived to ten, twenty, thirty, etcetera.

CADEN
Is that possible?

MADELINE
Which part?

(CONTINUED)

61 CONTINUED: (2)   61

>   CADEN
>   Any of it. Why did he kill
>   himself?

>   MADELINE
>   I don't know, why did you?

>   CADEN
>   What?

>   MADELINE
>   I said, why would you?

>   CADEN
>   Oh. I don't know.

62 INT. OLIVE'S ROOM - 2009 - NIGHT   62

Caden paces nervously. He sits on Olive's bed and jimmies open her diary with a screwdriver. He reads:

>   VOICE
>   Deer Diry. Thank you for being my
>   new best frend. My name is Olive
>   Cotard. I am for yers old. I like
>   choclit and --

63 INT. SCHENECTADY TOY STORE - 2009 - DAY   63

Caden looks at the toys.

>   VOICE
>   -- my favorite color is pink.

>   CLERK
>   Can I help you?

>   CADEN
>   I'm looking for a Christmas present
>   for my daughter. Something pink.

>   CLERK
>   How about this?

The clerk holds up a pink box with a picture of a nose on it.

>   CADEN
>   Yes. That's good.

64 OMITTED   64

65   INT. QUINCY'S - 2009 - DAY   65

Caden sits with Hazel. She seems somewhat distant.

                    CADEN
          The idea is to do a massive theater
          piece. Uncompromising, honest. I
          don't know what it is yet or how to
          do it, but it'll come. It'll
          reveal itself.

                    HAZEL
          Huh.

Pause.

                    CADEN
          Here's what I think theater is:
          it's the beginning of thought. The
          truth not yet spoken. It's a
          blackbird in winter. The moment
          before death. It's what a man
          feels after he's been clocked in
          the jaw. It's love... in all its
          messiness. And I want all of us,
          players and audience alike, to soak
          in the communal bath of it, the
          mikvah, as the Jews call it. We're
          all in the same water, after all,
          soaking in our very menstrual blood
          and nocturnal emissions. This is
          what I want to try to give people,
          Hazel. And I want your help.

Hazel just stares. The food arrives. Caden looks at his
plate and concentrates.

                    HAZEL
          What are you doing?

                    CADEN
          Salivating.
              (pause)
          I have to concentrate.
              (pause)
          Biofeedback training.

                    HAZEL
          Huh.

                    CADEN
          So I was wondering if you'll help.

                                              (CONTINUED)

                    HAZEL
            In your box office?

                    CADEN
            No. Like as my assistant.

                    HAZEL
            I'm not sure I can work with you,
            Caden. I'm kind of angry.

                    CADEN
            I just want to normalize it, Hazel.
            I think we'd have fun together.

He swallows some food then concentrates. She watches him.

                    CADEN (CONT'D)
            I miss you.

He concentrates some more. She stares at him.

                    CADEN (CONT'D)
            I'm digesting.

                    HAZEL
            It's really disturbing.

INT. TINY, CRAMPED REHEARSAL HALL - 2009 - DAY

Caden, beads of sweat on his forehead, sits with a large group of actors, Tom, Claire, and Davis from <u>Salesman</u> among them. No one speaks. Finally, Caden clears his throat.

                    CADEN
            We'll start by talking honestly.
            Out of that a piece of theater will
            evolve. I'll begin.
                (long pause)
            I've been thinking a lot about
            dying lately.

                    CLAIRE
            You're going to be fine, sweetie.

                    CADEN
            I appreciate that, Claire, but --

        CLAIRE   CADEN
Well, you are. You poor   regardless of how this
thing.   particular thing works itself
                                out, I will be dying. So
                                will you.

                                                (CONTINUED)

CONTINUED:

CLAIRE
Caden!

CADEN
So will everyone here. And I want to explore that unflinchingly.

There is a long silence as everyone looks uncomfortable.

CADEN (CONT'D)
We are all hurtling toward death.
(silence)
Yet here we are, for the moment, alive. Each of us knowing we will die; each of us secretly believing we won't.

Nobody says anything for a long moment.

CLAIRE
It's brilliant. It's brilliant. It's everything. It's Karamazov.

INT. CADEN AND ADELE'S BEDROOM - WINTER 2010 - NIGHT

Caden is in bed, reading Olive's diary.

VOICE
Dear diary. Germany is wonderful! So many friends here. My new dads are great and handsome. And brilliant directors of theater.

Caden grimaces in pain for a moment. His mouth bleeds. He dials the phone.

HAZEL'S ANSWERING MACHINE
It's Hazel. Leave a message or don't. Your dime.

CADEN
Hi. I haven't heard from you so I thought I'd say hi. Hi, Hazel!

He giggles crazily, coughs, then hangs up, embarrassed, grimaces once more, then dials again.

CLAIRE (PHONE VOICE)
Hello?

CADEN
Hi, Claire, it's Caden.

CLAIRE (PHONE VOICE)
Hi! I was just thinking about you!

(CONTINUED)

67   CONTINUED: 67

                         CADEN
               Yeah? Um, I was calling to say hi,
               chat about today maybe.

                         CLAIRE (PHONE VOICE)
               Hi! Here you are, on my phone!

                         CADEN
               Yeah. Do you maybe want to get a
               drink or something? It's late so --

                         CLAIRE
               Yeah! Yeah yeah yeah!

68   INT. QUINCY'S - 2010 - NIGHT   68

      Caden waits in a booth, nursing a martini, watching people
      walk in, but not Claire. After a bit, Hazel enters with
      Derek from the burning house. She's laughing and doesn't see
      Caden. He slinks back into the booth. They sit at a table
      not far from Caden, who can hear their conversation.

                         HAZEL   DEREK
                 (giggly)   I'm just asking.
               Stop!

                         HAZEL
               You are so obnoxious!

                         DEREK
               You're so obnoxious.

                         HAZEL
               Yeah, well, you find it awfully
               charming. My obnoxiousity.

                         DEREK
               Obnoxiousity is not a word.

                         HAZEL
               You don't want to cross me.

                         DEREK
               Don't I?

                         HAZEL
               No. Because you like me so much.

                         DEREK
               True. I like your obnoxiousity.

                                                              (CONTINUED)

HAZEL
And my use of the word "obnoxiousity."

DEREK
Yes.

HAZEL
Yes. You're delicious in your acquiescence.

Claire enters, looks for Caden. She spots Hazel first.

HAZEL (CONT'D)
Hi, Claire.

CLAIRE
Hi...!

HAZEL
Hazel.

CLAIRE
Of course. Hazel. I knew that! Duh! The box office.

HAZEL
Yes, I'm the box office.

CLAIRE
How are you?

HAZEL
Wonderful! You?

CLAIRE
Fine, thanks. I was supposed to meet Caden here. You know Mr. Cotard, right?

HAZEL
Yes, I recall Mr. Cotard.

Hazel looks around now, too. Both spot Caden at the same time. He smiles and waves and approaches.

CADEN
Oh, hey.

HAZEL	CLAIRE
Hi, Caden.	Hi, Caden.

(CONTINUED)

                    CADEN (CONT'D)
          Hi, Hazel. Hi, Claire.

                    HAZEL
          This is Derek.

          CADEN   CLAIRE
Hi, Derek.   Hi, Derek.

                    HAZEL (CONT'D)
          Hi, Derek.

                    DEREK
          Hi.

                    CADEN
          How's everything, Haze... ul?

                    HAZEL
          Great, Cade. En.

          CADEN   CLAIRE
Good. It's good to see you.   (awkwardly)
                                    Reunion night! How lovely!

                    HAZEL (CONT'D)
          Yes.

          HAZEL   CADEN
So --   We'll leave you be.

                    HAZEL (CONT'D)
          Yeah, okay. Thanks. Derek and I --

          CADEN   HAZEL
No, of course. It was nice   Take care.
seeing you.

Caden and Claire go to Caden's booth.

                    CLAIRE
          That was awkward.

                    CADEN
          Yeah, I guess.

Caden steals glances at Hazel, chatting animatedly, throughout his conversation with Claire. He hears occasional snippets.

(CONTINUED)

CLAIRE
Let's talk about our project. I'm so excited about it.

CADEN
Really? Why?

CLAIRE
I just think it's... brave. I feel like I'm going to be part of a revolution. I keep thinking Artaud. I keep thinking Krapp's Last Tape. Grotowski, for Christ's sake!

CADEN
I don't know what I'm doing.

CLAIRE
But that's what's so refreshing. I mean, how much prepackaged ...

HAZEL
... cryptology...

CLAIRE
... theater can we take as a country? Y'know? Knowing that you don't know is the first and most essential step to knowing. Y'know?

CADEN
I don't know.

CLAIRE
I'm proud of you.

HAZEL
Ptolemy was the first to divide the day into 24...

CLAIRE
So tell me what you want from me?

CADEN
Hmm?

CLAIRE
From my character.

CADEN
Oh. Well, we'll build it over time together. Find a real person, maybe, to model it after.

CLAIRE
That sounds fun.

HAZEL
...hairstyle called a beaver tail. It's a loop of hair...

(CONTINUED)

CLAIRE
That Hazel girl is kind of interesting, maybe. As a model.

CADEN
Um, yeah. Something to think about. Sure. Although --

CLAIRE
Y'know, why is she still working in a box office at her age?

CADEN
I don't know. Probably not that interesting.

CLAIRE
There's got to be a story there. Did she want to be an actress but lacked confidence? You seem distracted.

CADEN
Yeah. Could be. We'll talk about it.

CADEN (CONT'D)
No. I have these health issues.

CLAIRE
It's late.

HAZEL
... and the jet, it exploded, and she was sent plummeting.

CADEN (CONT'D)
Um...

CLAIRE
Well, we can talk more tomorrow maybe.

CADEN (CONT'D)
I'm sorry.
    (pause)
When I get tired I have to remember to breathe. It's a new thing. My autonomic functions are failing.

CLAIRE
Poor darling. It's fine.

CADEN
I'm just ...

CLAIRE
    (grabbing his hand)
Shh. Shh. Shh. Shh. Shh.

Claire leads Caden past Hazel and Derek, deep in conversation, heads close together.

HAZEL
Whitrow says, "If a mind is regarded to be a memory-based process of integration..."

69 EXT. DOWNTOWN SCHENECTADY STREET - WINTER 2010 - NIGHT 69

Caden and Claire walk. It's bitterly cold. They pass a store window advertising a Presidents Day sale. The female mannequins are dressed as Lincoln and Washington. Caden glances at their star-spangled bikini-bottomed crotches.

> CLAIRE
> My mother died last night.

> CADEN
> My God. I'm so sorry. What are you doing out?

> CLAIRE
> Ugh, I couldn't deal with my sisters. It's like living in a Heironymous Bosch painting.

> CADEN
> Oh. I see. Well, um, What happened to your mother, if I could ask? I mean, God, that's an awful thing to ask. I'm sorry. I don't mean to -- It's just that, I'm --

> CLAIRE
> Oh, this is me. No, it's okay. She fell. Slipped in her bathroom. Hit her head. It actually split in half. Horrible.

They stop at a small hatchback with a cow painted on it.

> CADEN
> In half?

> CLAIRE
> Yes. Well, it was nice meeting you. Did I say "meeting"? Ugh, I'm such an idiot.

> CADEN
> Slip of the tongue is all.

> CLAIRE
> Freudian slip.

> CADEN
> I don't know how it's Freudian.

> CLAIRE
> Y'know. Like "*meet*"? To *meet*?

(CONTINUED)

                            CADEN
                  Oh. Well, I'm sorry about your
                  mother. In half?

                            CLAIRE
                  It's okay. It's life. It's --

Claire's face contorts into a horrifying, paralyzed grimace.

                            CADEN
                  What is it? What?

She weeps silently, with gaping mouth. Caden awkwardly
embraces her. She remains stiff.

                            CADEN (CONT'D)
                  Do you want me to drive you home?

She shakes her head "no" over and over. Then she looks in at
her reflection in the car window.

                            CLAIRE
                  Sometimes when I cry, I watch
                  myself so I can remember how it
                  looks for future roles. It's
                  horrible. I hate myself.

                            CADEN
                  It's okay. Everyone does that.
                  It's -- is there anything I can do?

70   INT. CHURCH - 2010 - DAY   70

Caden sits with Claire and a large congregation. She rests
her hand on Caden's.

                            MINISTER
                  ...there she met Ralph Keene. They
                  fell in love, married, and soon
                  their first child, Claire was born.

The minister's voice goes under.

                            CLAIRE
                       (crying whisper to Caden)
                  I used to be a baby.

                            CADEN
                  I'm so sorry.

                                                        (CONTINUED)

70   CONTINUED: 70

                    CLAIRE
          I was a baby girl with hair of spun
          gold, the prettiest baby anyone had
          ever seen. One day the townsfolk,
          who were jealous of my beauty,
          decided to steal me away.

71   OMITTED   71

72   INT. CLAIRE'S BEDROOM (SCHENECTADY APT.) - 2010 - DAY   72

       Curtains drawn, the room glows with afternoon sunlight.
       Caden sits on the bed. Claire enters naked from the
       bathroom, brushing her teeth and talking.

            CLAIRE   CADEN
       There was a knock at the   God, you're beautiful.
       door.

                    CLAIRE
               (sits on bed next to him)
          It was a bearded old man.

       Caden can hold out no longer. He kisses her. They fall back
       on the bed. He kisses her all over as she continues to tell
       the story. Her voice becomes irresistibly melodious.

                    CLAIRE (CONT'D)
          He said to me, "young lady, I have
          in my satchel a ring. Whomever
          possesses it will receive all the
          magic of the woodland sprites."

            CADEN   CLAIRE
       (eyes blurring, head   (spreading her legs)
       lolling, breathing her   "You can have this ring if
       in)   you promise me one thing."
       I have to fuck you. I have   "Anything," I whispered in
       to.   his ear.

       Caden and Claire are having sex now.

                    CLAIRE (CONT'D)
          He said, "There is one more thing.
          You must never tell anyone what you
          promised me. If you do, you will
          die."

73   INT. CLAIRE'S BATHROOM (SCHENECTADY APT.) - 2010 - DAY   73

       Claire sits on the toilet and pees.

                                                         (CONTINUED)

73 CONTINUED: 73

                    CLAIRE
          So I used my new power to kill all
          the townsfolk. Horrible,
          humiliating deaths. I was reunited
          with my family. And I lived
          happily ever after, doing only good
          with my new powers.

Caden cries and rests his head on her thigh.

                    CLAIRE (CONT'D)
          Why are you crying, honey?

                    CADEN
          I'm so in love with you.

Claire smiles, strokes his hair.

                    CADEN (CONT'D)
          I have problems, Claire. I'm still
          attached to my wife. I have also --
          I have also -- feelings for Hazel.

                    CLAIRE
              (wiping)
          Really? Hazel? Oh. Really? Our
          Hazel? That's really interesting.
          I must've picked that up
          unconsciously. Wow. Boy. Gosh.

                    CADEN
          I've left them behind. I've gone
          somewhere without them. I'm guilty
          of so much.

                    CLAIRE
          It's okay. We'll be fine. You're
          with me now. We'll be good.

74   INT. CHURCH - 2010 - DAY   74

Caden and Claire get married. Caden is saying his vows.

                    CADEN
          There will be no other before you.

75   INT. SCHENECTADY POST OFFICE - WINTER 2010 - DAY   75

Caden stands in line with a gift-wrapped box addressed to
Olive. The clerks at the counter wear Santa hats and beards.

76 INT. TINY, CRAMPED REHEARSAL HALL - 2011 - DAY 76

Actors piled in. Claire sits at a makeshift "box-office."
Davis approaches. Caden circles the action. There are
ponderous pauses.

DAVIS	CLAIRE
I'd like to buy a ticket.	Okay. That'll be forty dollars.

DAVIS	CLAIRE
Okay. Forty dollars it is.	Okay. Here's your ticket.

                    CADEN
          Okay, hold it. We're not really --
          I think we need to work on your
          characters individually. We need
          to investigate, to really discover
          the essence of each being. Davis,
          I'll start with you.

Caden walks off with Davis. Claire seethes.

77 INT. CLAIRE'S KITCHEN (SCHENECTADY APT.) - WINTER 2011 - 77
    NIGHT

Claire chops vegetables. Caden feeds a baby. Christmas
decorations are up.

                    CLAIRE
Davis, I'll start with you. There's a difference between
favoring me and pretending we've never met. I mean, we had
Ariel, I think people know we've fucked.

CADEN	CLAIRE
That's not the point.	Apparently not. I would've guessed you were sleeping with Davis.

CADEN	CLAIRE
We'll talk about your character after we get Ariel to bed. Okay?	Maybe you are. I just want to feel what we used to feel. Y'know?

78 INT. CLAIRE'S BEDROOM (SCHENECTADY APT.)- WINTER 2011 - 78
    NIGHT

Claire sits on the bed and seems almost in a trance. She
looks haggard and her cheeks are tear-stained.

                                              (CONTINUED)

78 CONTINUED: 78

                    CLAIRE
          She's 36. Works in a theater box
          office. She had acting aspirations
          but lacked the confidence to pursue
          them. Her life is passing by. She
          is alone. She's old and ugly --

                    CADEN
          I think you should pick another
          subject. Other than Hazel.

                    CLAIRE
          Sacred ground?

                    CADEN
          No. It's just. I don't feel like
          there's enough there.

Claire thinks for a moment.

                    CLAIRE
          I suppose not. She is limited.
          Okay. There's this single mother
          who lives downstairs. I find her
          really deep and sad.

                    CADEN
          Tell me.

                    CLAIRE
          I'm 42. I have a small child and   *
          no husband. I work long hours as a
          cashier at a mini-mart. Sometimes
          I worry my child will not even
          recognize me when I come home --

Claire cries like she did when her mother died. Ariel cries.

                    CLAIRE (CONT'D)   *
          Check on her. Please, sweetie.
          I'm arriving at something.

79   INT. CLAIRE'S LIVING ROOM (SCHENECTADY APT.) - WINTER 2011 - 79
      NIGHT

Ariel sleeps in a crib in the corner of the living room.

                                                          (CONTINUED)

79   CONTINUED: 79

Caden sits on a tiny chair, thumbing through a magazine. Claire weeps off-screen. Caden sees an article entitled "Flower Girl", featuring a photo of a naked Olive, smiling, her body covered from neck to ankle in tattoos of flowers. The article begins, "Ten year old Olive Wittgart of Berlin is the first child in human history with a full body tattoo... " Caden stares in disbelief. Claire pokes her head in. Her eyes are red.

        CLAIRE   CADEN
Caden, I've made a   I have to go find my
breakthrough. This woman is   daughter.
beautiful. I've got --

        CLAIRE
Your daughter is right here.

        CADEN
My real daughter.

        CLAIRE   CADEN
What?   My first daughter. Olive.
                                          I've got to find her.

        CLAIRE
Please don't do this to us.

        CADEN
She's tattooed!

        CLAIRE
     (revealing massive tattoo
      on back)
Everyone's tattooed!

        CADEN   CLAIRE
I've never seen that before.   You have responsibilities.

        CADEN
I'll be quick. I'll do it quick.

        CLAIRE
Everyone's tattooed. Please.

80   INT. PLANE - 2011 - NIGHT   80

It's dark; most people are sleeping. Caden reads <u>Getting Better</u>.

(CONTINUED)

80   CONTINUED: 80

                    VOICE
          Redundancy is fluid. Life moves to
          the south. There is only the now.

                    MADELINE
          Hi.

He sees Madeline sitting across the aisle. She is different,
sexier in make-up and a tight dress.

                    MADELINE (CONT'D)
          When you cancelled, it freed me up.
          So I'm traveling, too! Yippee!

                    CADEN
          I'm not sure I'm getting the book.

                    MADELINE
          But it's getting you. You're
          almost non-recognizable now.

Madeline spreads her legs a bit and smiles at Caden. He
nervously grins, goes back to his book. He reads:

                    VOICE
          I offer my flower to you and you
          deny it. This book is over.

He turns the page. Blank. The rest of the book is blank.
He looks over at Madeline. She is watching a movie.

81   EXT. BERLIN STREET - 2011 - DAY   81

Caden wanders a dirty store-front street looking for an
address. He finds it. An art gallery. He enters.

                                                                      *

82   INT. GALLERY - 2011 - DAY   82

The walls are hung with hundreds of Adele's tiny paintings.

          CADEN   GERMAN WOMAN
I don't speak German. I was -   Yes yes. I may help you,
-                                Mister?

                                                        (CONTINUED)

CONTINUED:

> CADEN
> I'm looking for Adele Cotard.

> GERMAN WOMAN
> Yes. We must not give addresses or other personal informations.

> CADEN
> I'm her husband.

> GERMAN WOMAN
> No. You are not her husbands, which is named Gunther und Heinz.

EXT. OUTDOOR CAFE - 2015 - DAY

Caden sits nursing a coffee. Maria approaches and sits down.

> CADEN
> You're here, too?

> MARIA
> I live with Adele and Olive and Gunther und Heinz and Uschi and Britt. I'm everyone's nanny.

> CADEN
> I want to see my daughter.

> MARIA
> They sent me.

> CADEN
> They? And who the fuck are Uschi and Britt?

> MARIA
> They decided it's not time to see you yet.

> CADEN
> Maria, I can't believe Adele got her tattooed like that. I mean --

> MARIA
> I did that. Olive's my project.

> CADEN
> She's a four year old!

(CONTINUED)

83 CONTINUED: 83

                    MARIA
          She's almost over eleven now.
          She's my muse. I love her.

Caden stares at her for a moment, then lunges. He punches
her repeatedly as she tries to get away. She throws a punch
which connects with the side of his head and knocks him down.
She hurries off.

                    CADEN
          What'd you do to my family? What'd
          you do to my daughter?

                    MARIA (IN GERMAN)
          Screw you, Caden. Faggot! FAGGOT!

She turns down an alley. Caden, a half-block behind, hurries
to the alley. She's gone. He walks through, looking for
her. It's dark. Trash cans and garbage. He spots an
unopened box next to the trash. It's pink with a picture of
a nose on it. Caden drops to his knees and weeps. No tears
come out. His eyes are dry and red. He pulls a vial of
artificial tears from his pockets and moistens his eyes.
Suddenly his breathing becomes wildly erratic.

A84 EXT. GERMAN HOSPITAL - 2015 - DAY   A84

     Caden limps up to the hospital.

84   INT. GERMAN HOSPITAL ROOM - 2015 - DAY   84

     German words painted on the walls. Caden, in his underwear,
     lies on a metal table in a cold room, while an old man in
     white military jacket examines him, pressing on his body in
     various places. The man is silent except for slow, long
     inhalations and exhalations through his nose. When he is
     through he leaves the room without saying a word. Caden lies
     there, not sure what he's supposed to do. After a while, he
     gets up and opens the door, looks both ways down the empty
     hall. He closes the door, sits in a plastic chair and waits.

85   INT. PLANE - 2015 - NIGHT   85

     Caden sits. A tube runs from his nostril to a small whirring
     machine on his lap. A frail old man sits next to him.

                    OLD MAN
          Death comes faster than you think.

86 EXT. NEW YORK CITY STREET - 2015 - DAY 86

Caden, walking with a realtor, approaches a warehouse in a very old, decrepit, and abandoned-looking part of town.

> CADEN
> Yeah, I want to bring my production to New York. To get it seen. By people, you know, who matter. The sooner the better.

> REALTOR
> Well, this theater is centrally located. Heart of the theater district. So... great for plays.

> CADEN
> Yeah?

> REALTOR
> Yeah. Very much so.

87 INT. WAREHOUSE - 2015 - DAY 87

It's massive, empty, old, and dirty. Caden inspects it while the agent watches from a distance.

> REALTOR
> (echoey and far away)
> Lots of room for seats over here.

88 OMITTED 88

89 INT. WAREHOUSE - 2016 - DAY 89

It's been scrubbed. There are small squared-off "apartment" areas, with actors in each, going about their days. A couple sleeps in a bed in one, in another there is a conversation between people over dinner, a man watches television alone in one, etc. There are at least fifteen configurations of people with a reel-to-reel tape recorders in each set-up. Caden walks from one to the other, eavesdropping, followed by an assistant, Michael. He stops at Claire's "apartment." She is ironing and watching a daytime soap, which is a closed-circuit TV. The actors in the soap are across the warehouse in another apartment. Ariel sits in a highchair and plays with a bowl of Cheerios. She is about two and a half.

> ARIEL
> Daddy! Daddy is mine!

> CADEN
> Daddy can't play now, honey.

> CLAIRE
> Daddy doesn't live with us anymore, baby. He had to find himself.

(CONTINUED)

89 CONTINUED: 89

Claire shoots daggers at Caden and goes back to ironing.

90 EXT. BUS SHELTER (NEAR WAREHOUSE) - 2016 - NIGHT   90

Caden sits in the fluorescent shelter. He looks at a poster for a movie called <u>Little Winky and Caden</u>, which features Caden in an embrace with a muscular skinhead. The movie is "Posthumously Written" by The Late Horace Azpiazu.

Caden's leg starts to twitch, and he goes into convulsions.

91 OMITTED   91

92 INT. EXAMINATION ROOM - 2017 - NIGHT   92

An old doctor examines Caden's shaking leg.

          DOCTOR
I can't argue with further testing.

          CADEN
Ok, you're a doctor, right? Am I dying? Can you tell me that?

          DOCTOR
No.

          CADEN
No, you can't tell me?

          DOCTOR
I can't tell you.

          DOCTOR (CONT'D)
You can't tell me if you can't tell me?

          DOCTOR (CONT'D)
No.

93 EXT. NYC STREET - 2017 - DAY   93

Caden walks along, his leg shaking. He spots Hazel looking in a store window. He just watches her for a while. She sees him in the store window reflection. She turns.

          HAZEL
Caden! I was wondering if I was going to bump into you!

She gives him a hug, notices his shaking leg.

(CONTINUED)

CADEN
What are you doing here? You look great.

HAZEL
Oh, thanks. You... I --

CADEN
New haircut?

HAZEL
Um, yeah. For a while now.

CADEN
What are you doing in New York?

HAZEL
Oh. I'm here with Derek and the boys. Mini-vacation! You know.

CADEN
The boys?

HAZEL
Yeah. I thought you knew.

CADEN
Ah. Congratulations.

HAZEL
Yeah. Thanks.

CADEN
How old?

HAZEL
Five. Twins. Robert and Daniel and Allan.

CADEN
Ah. Yes.
    (pause)
Nice names. Where are they?

HAZEL
Oh. Derek took them to Natural History. So I could shop.

CADEN
Ah.

HAZEL
Nice to see you, Caden. How are things?

(CONTINUED)

93   CONTINUED: (2)   93

                          CADEN
                Y'know. I was with Claire. We
                have a daughter, but we're
                separated now. How about with
                you?

                          HAZEL
                Good. The kids are wonderful. I
                have a great job at Lens Shapers.

                          CADEN
                Great. You wear a lab coat?

                          HAZEL
                It's so good to see you. I should
                run. I want to get some shopping
                in. We're meeting back at the
                hotel at three. Then sushi!

                          CADEN
                Okay. Good seeing you, Hazel.

     Hazel smiles and waves and turns to head into the store.
     Caden watches after her.

94   EXT. HOTEL - 2017 - DAY   94

     Caden watches Hazel, Derek, and the boys enter the hotel.

A95 INT. HOTEL HALLWAY - 2017 - DAY   A95

     Caden trails behind Hazel and her family, laughing and
     enjoying each other as they head down the hall to their room.
     When they enter their room, Caden just continues down the
     hall toward the window at the far end. Without hesitation he
     opens it and begins to climb out. A man steps out of his
     room, sees Caden, grabs him and wrestles him to the ground.
     The gaunt man watches from down the hall.

95   INT. CADEN AND ADELE'S HOUSE - 2017 - NIGHT   95

     Caden pulls Olive's journal from under his pillow and reads
     from somewhere in the middle.

                          OLIVE'S VOICE
                     (with German accent)
                How I love Maria! She is so much
                more of a father than Caden ever
                was, with his drinking and
                unfortunate body odor and rotting
                teeth. I could only loathe him and
                perhaps pity him. But Maria!

                                                         (CONTINUED)

95 CONTINUED: 95

Caden blots his sopping brow and gums, sniffs under his arms.

96 INT. HALLWAY (CLAIRE'S NYC APT.) - FALL 2018 - NIGHT   96

Caden, now walking with a cane, approaches an apartment door. There's a sad pilgrim cut-out taped to it. He knocks.

      CLAIRE (O.S.)
  Yes?

      CADEN
  It's me.

   ARIEL (O.S.)   CLAIRE (O.S.)
Daddy, Daddy!   What, Caden?

      CADEN (CONT'D)
  I want to come back. I want to
  take care of you and Olive. Ariel.

There's silence then the door opens. Claire is crying.

      CLAIRE
  I just want you to love us.

Caden hugs her. Ariel hugs Caden's good leg.

      ARIEL
  Why does you have a canes, Daddy?

97 INT. CLAIRE'S BEDROOM (NYC APARTMENT) - 2018 - NIGHT   97

Caden and Claire in bed having sex. The gaunt man stands on the fire escape peering in. Ariel watches from the doorway. The phone rings. Claire cranes her neck and looks at the clock. The gaunt man and Ariel both step out of view.

      CLAIRE
  It's 3:30. For crying out fuck.

Caden answers the phone.

      CADEN
  Hello? What's wrong? Okay. Okay.

Caden hangs up. Claire kisses Caden's neck.

      CADEN (CONT'D)
  My father died.

      CLAIRE
  Oh, baby.

          (CONTINUED)

97 CONTINUED: 97

                    CADEN
          His body was riddled with cancer.
          He didn't even know. He went in
          because his finger hurt.

                    CLAIRE
          It's okay, baby. It's going to be
          okay. Let me make you feel better.

Claire begins kissing her way down Caden's chest.

                    CADEN
          They said he suffered horribly.
          That he called out for me right
          before he died. They said he said
          he regretted his life. They said
          he said a lot of things. Too many
          to recount. They said it was the
          longest and saddest deathbed speech
          any of them had ever heard.

98   EXT. CEMETERY - 2018 - DAY   98

Caden, Claire, and Ariel stand with Caden's mother as a child-sized coffin is lowered into the ground.

                    MOTHER
          There was so little left of him.
          They had to fill the coffin with
          cotton balls to keep him from
          rattling around.

99   INT. CADEN'S MOTHER'S HOUSE - 2018 - DAY   99

Crowded with mourners. People chat and eat. Claire and Caden, on the couch holding hands, chat with a fat lady.

                    CADEN
          Excuse me, I have to use the
          bathroom.

100 EXT. CADEN'S MOTHER'S BACK DECK - 2018 - A FEW MOMENTS   100
     LATER

Caden dials his cell phone.

                    CADEN
          Hey.

                                                              INTERCUT WITH:

A101 INT. BURNING HOUSE - 2018 - SAME   A101

Hazel is on her phone.

                    HAZEL (PHONE VOICE)
          Caden?

                    CADEN
          I had to talk to you. My father
          died.

                    HAZEL
          Oh no. Oh, Caden. I'm so sorry.

          CADEN   HAZEL
Thanks. I know.   Are you at your mom's?

                    CADEN
          Yeah. With Claire and Ariel.

          HAZEL   CADEN
Oh. I see.   I'm back with Claire.

Pause.

                    HAZEL
          Yes, I got that.

          CADEN   HAZEL
I'm sorry.   What are you sorry about?

                    CADEN
          I don't know. You got quiet. I
          thought I should say something.

                    HAZEL
          You thought you should say
          something. That's lovely. That's
          what makes our relationship so
          special. The obligation.

                    CADEN
          What am I supposed to do, Hazel? I
          have a kid with her. You have
          twins with Derek. Three twins.
          It's confusing!

          HAZEL   CADEN
You're not supposed to do   I really miss you.
anything.

                                              (CONTINUED)

A101 CONTINUED: A101

                         HAZEL
              Yeah, I guess that's what happens
              when you have a kid with somebody
              else. You having sex with her?

              CADEN   HAZEL
         Hazel...   I'm asking you a question.
                                     Did you have sex with her now
                                     that you're back together?

                         CADEN
              Yes. Of course. I mean, what --

                         HAZEL
              I have to go. I'm sorry about your
              dad. That's awful news.

                         CADEN
              Hazel, please, I can't bear it if
              you go.

                         HAZEL
              I have to. I'm going out. I have
              to get ready. Everything's fine.

                         CADEN
              I need to use a cane now.
                   (pause)
              Okay. Take care.

    Hazel hangs up. Caden sits there.

101   OMITTED   101

102   OMITTED   102

103   INT. WAREHOUSE - CITY SET - 2020 - DAY   103

    A rehearsal in progress. The shells of apartment buildings
    have been built. The actors, who previously had been spread
    out on the floor of the warehouse, are now perched on
    scaffolding in various apartment spaces. Caden, followed by
    Michael, surveys the scene by climbing up and down ladders.
    It's difficult to manage with his cane.

104   INT. CLAIRE KITCHEN (NYC APARTMENT) - 2021 - LATE NIGHT   104

    Caden reads Olive's diary.

                         OLIVE'S GERMAN VOICE
              Today I felt a wetness between my
              legs.
                   (MORE)

                                                          (CONTINUED)

104 CONTINUED: 104

                    OLIVE'S GERMAN VOICE (CONT'D)
                Maria explained to me now I am a
                woman. And being a woman is
                wonderful with Maria to guide me.

105 EXT. BERLIN STREET - 2022 - DAY   105

     Overcast. Caden wanders. Walls are plastered with posters
     of "Flower Girl." It's Olive, early 20's, very sexy and
     naked. There is an address and a date. Seems to be some
     sort of concert.

106 INT. LOBBY - 2022 - NIGHT   106

     Caden waits on a long line behind a bunch of men.

107 INT DARK SMALL ROOM - NIGHT   107

     Caden sits by himself in a cramped space. A light switches
     on behind scarred Plexiglas. Olive dances naked. Caden
     tries to get her attention by banging on the glass but she
     can't see him. A bouncer enters and beats Caden up.

108 INT. CLAIRE'S BEDROOM (NYC APARTMENT) - 2022 - MORNING   108

     Caden, bruised, lies in bed while Claire hurries past,
     getting dressed.

                    CLAIRE   CADEN
          Get out of bed.   I'm depressed.

                          CLAIRE
                The cry of the North American
                Caden.

                          CADEN
                I'd just like a little sympathy.

                          CLAIRE
                I'll save my sympathy for the
                eighty million people with avian
                flu, the Tsunami victims in Puerto
                Rico, the countless millennia dead
                from... how *fucked* it all is.

                          CADEN
                Millennia dead? What? And since
                when do you care about anything?

                          CLAIRE
                I care every day about things! I
                care about us! ... Y'know?!

                                                              (CONTINUED)

                    ARIEL
          Why do Daddy be sad now?

109   EXT. BURNING HOUSE - 2023 - DAY   109

The neighborhood seems abandoned and overgrown. Caden is parked down the block and watches Hazel's house. Soon Hazel and Derek walk by. Derek says something and Hazel laughs delightedly. Caden is in agony. He rolls down his window.

                    CADEN
          Hazel!

Hazel and Derek turn.

          HAZEL   CADEN
Caden, what are you doing   Sorry. Can I talk to you?
here?   Please?

Hazel kisses Derek, whispers something in his ear. They share a giggle. Derek waves at Caden and heads into the burning house. Hazel approaches Caden's car.

                    CADEN (CONT'D)
          Tell me what to do.

          HAZEL   CADEN
Caden, everyone has to figure I want you to look at me like
out their own life. Y'know?   you used to.

                    HAZEL
          Oh, honey, I can't anymore.

                    CADEN
               (crying)
          I'm sorry. I'm sorry. I screwed
          everything up. I don't have any
          courage. I'm sorry.

                    HAZEL
          It's okay. I'm okay.

                    CADEN
          I don't want you to be okay. I
          mean, I do but it rips my guts out.

                    HAZEL
          I'll always be your friend. I'll
          help you through any way I can.

                    CADEN
          I'll help you through, too.

                                                    (CONTINUED)

109   CONTINUED: 109

                        HAZEL
              Caden, I'm fine. I have Derek.

110   INT. WAREHOUSE - 2023 - DAY   110

    Caden stands with his cane before the group of seated actors.
    The actors wait patiently as Caden finishes a coughing fit.

                        CADEN
              I won't settle for anything less
              than the brutal truth. Brutal!
              Each day I'll hand you a scrap of
              paper. It'll tell you what
              happened to you that day. "You
              felt a lump in your breast. You
              looked at your wife and saw a
              stranger." Etcetera.

              TOM   CADEN
    Caden, when are we going to   And I'm not excusing myself
    get an audience in here?   from this either. I will
    It's been seventeen years.   have someone play me, to
                                      delve into the murky,
                                      cowardly depths of my lonely,
                                      fucked-up being. He'll get
                                      notes, too. And they will
                                      correspond to the "notes" I   *
                                      truly get each day from my
                                      God.

    The actors glance uncomfortably at Claire. She smiles
    apologetically.

111   OMITTED   111

112   EXT. NYC DEPARTMENT STORE - WINTER 2023 - DAY   112

    Caden walks by a Salvation Army Santa. Suddenly the Santa
    claws spastically at his beard. He rips it off revealing a
    tortured, blue face. He gasps for air, and dies.

113   INT. HAZEL'S CAR - 2024 - DAY   113

    Hazel sits in her parked car and talks on her cellphone.
    Little kids in costumes walk by. A little girl walks by in a
    "nude" body suit with Olive's tattoos all over it.

                        HAZEL
              They fired me. I caused an
              outbreak of conjunctivitis.
                        (MORE)

                                                              (CONTINUED)

113   CONTINUED: 113

                        HAZEL (CONT'D)
              I didn't wash my hands. I had pink
              eye hands! Pink hands!

                                              INTERCUT WITH:

A114   INT. WAREHOUSE - 2024 - SAME   A114

     Caden sits at his desk, talking on his cell phone.

                        CADEN
              Oh God.

                        HAZEL
              I didn't wash my hands!

                        HAZEL (CONT'D)
              I'm a stupid cow! I don't have
              anything to show for being on this
              planet. And this fucking private
              Christian school is killing us.
              It's not cheap. It's Derek's
              thing. I don't believe in that
              shit. Y'know? Try to be a good
              person. That's all there is. I'm
              sorry. I'm talking too much. Do
              you have anything for me, Caden?

              CADEN   HAZEL
     Um, I have an assistant,   Please, Caden. Everything is
     Hazel. And there's no box   falling apart. I miss you.
     office yet.   There are problems at home.
                                    I'm worthless. I'm fat.
                                    What am I going to do?
                                    Nobody laughs at my jokes the
                                    way you did.

114   INT. WAREHOUSE - AUDITION CORNER - 2025 - LATER   114

     The actors are in their apartments living their lives. Caden
     is in the far corner of the space, at a little sectioned-off
     area. There are a half-dozen actors sitting on folding
     chairs outside the partition. They all resemble Caden,
     except one very tall one. Hazel steps around the partition.

                        HAZEL
              Sammy Barnathan?

     Sammy Barnathan stands. He is the gaunt man we've seen
     following Caden. Hazel leads him to Caden. Caden stands.

                                                          (CONTINUED)

                    HAZEL (CONT'D)   SAMMY
        This is Sammy Barnathan.   I don't have a resume or
                                           picture. I've never worked
                                           as an actor.

                              CADEN
                    Good. Tell me why you're here.

                              SAMMY
                    I've been following you for twenty
                    years. So I knew about this
                    audition. Because I follow you.

Caden, hiding is nervousness, nods.

                              SAMMY (CONT'D)
                    I've learned everything about you
                    by following you. Hire me and you
                    will see who you truly are.

Caden stares at Sammy. Sammy stares back. There's fear in
Caden's eyes but he doesn't drop his gaze.

                              SAMMY (CONT'D)
                    Peek-a-boo.

Sammy transforms effortlessly into Caden.

                              SAMMY (CONT'D)
                    Okay, Hazel, I don't think we need
                    to talk to anyone else. This guy
                    has me down. I'm going to cast him
                    right now. Then maybe you and I
                    can get a drink and we can try to
                    figure out this thing between us.
                    Why I cried. I've never felt about
                    anyone the way I feel about you. I
                    want to fuck you until we merge
                    into a Chimera. A mythical beast
                    with penis and vagina eternally
                    fused, two pair of eyes that look
                    only at each other, lips ever
                    touching and one voice that
                    whispers to itself.

                              CADEN
                    Yes, okay. You've got the part.

Sammy nods and exits. Hazel follows him with her eyes.

                              HAZEL
                    He's good, Caden.

                                                    (CONTINUED)

                    CADEN
          Please don't fall in love with him.

                    HAZEL
          I only have eyes for you, dear.

115   INT. WAREHOUSE - 2025 - A FEW MOMENTS LATER   115

      Caden limps with his cane and a backpack toward the men's
      room door. His eyes are rheumy. He pushes open the door.

116   INT. WAREHOUSE - MEN'S ROOM - 2025 - CONTINUOUS   116

      The room is filthy. Flies buzz. The urinals are covered
      with slime. Caden enters a stall, pulls down his pants, and
      sits. He strains. When he is done, he looks at his stool.
      It's gray. He wipes and flushes, pulls up his pants and
      exits the stall. Sammy stands there.

                    SAMMY
          I've never seen your shit gray.

                    CADEN
          It's new.

      Sammy jots a note. Caden places his backpack on a sink. He
      looks at himself in the mirror, stalling.

                    SAMMY
          I know it's pill time. You don't
          need to hide from me.

      Caden opens his pack and pulls out a baggie full of pills.
      He takes them, one-by-one. Sammy watches and counts. When
      it's over, he speaks.

                    SAMMY (CONT'D)
          You're missing your Fosonex.

                CADEN   SAMMY
      No.   Check your bag.

      Caden pulls out books and notebooks and a sweater. The pill
      falls out of the sweater onto the grimy floor.

                    SAMMY (CONT'D)
          Fosonex, 2.5 mg.

      Caden picks the pill up off the floor. It's got grime on it.

                                                      (CONTINUED)

116   CONTINUED: 116

                    SAMMY (CONT'D)
               Swallow it anyway. It's important.
               Go on, sweetie.

          Caden looks at Sammy and swallows the pill.

                    SAMMY (CONT'D)
               Good boy.

117   EXT. NYC CITY STREET - 2025 - EVENING   117

          Caden exits the warehouse with Claire and Ariel, who is now
          five. Sammy walks alongside. There is a long line of people
          waiting to find out about tickets for the show.

                    MAN
               When is it opening?

                    CADEN
               When it's ready.

                    MAN
               We need to get in. It's bad out
               here.

          They move on, passing poor people waiting in line for food
          distributed from a military truck. There are sick people
          being herded into a scary bus marked "Fun Land." The guards
          wear surgical masks.

                    CADEN
               I was thinking of calling it
               <u>Simulacrum</u>. What do you think?

                    CLAIRE
               I don't know what it means.

                    ARIEL
               Can me have a nickel if I doesn't
               play with my pee-pee no more?

          A hovercraft glides down the street with searchlights.

                    CADEN
               How about <u>The Flawed Light of Love
               and Grief?</u>

                    CLAIRE
               I'm not sure.

          Sammy jots something in his book.

118 INT. CLAIRE'S BEDROOM (NYC APARTMENT) - 2025 - NIGHT 118

Caden and Claire have sex. Sammy watches from a chair in the corner. Ariel sits on his lap. They finish and Caden glances at Sammy.

119 EXT. CLAIRE'S FIRE ESCAPE (NYC APARTMENT) - WINTER 2025 - LATER 119

Caden and Sammy watch the city: fires in the distance. Human wailing. Christmas decorations in windows across the way. Occasional explosions. Claire pokes her head out.

> CLAIRE
> I'm going to work in my journal. You guys need anything?

> CADEN
> No, thanks.

> SAMMY
> No, thanks, Claire.

> CADEN
> Claire? I want you to drop your study of Mrs. Kranstein.

> CLAIRE
> Caden --

> CADEN
> I want you to play yourself. Sammy's going to move into your apartment set as me.

> CLAIRE
> It's just that I've made such enormous strides as Jocelyn and --

> CADEN
> As the vision reveals itself, we all have to be willing to adapt, honey.

> SAMMY
> It'd be my honor to play your husband, Claire. You're an amazing actress. I saw you in Bernarda Alba last year at The Roundabout.

> CLAIRE
> Yeah? That was a fun play. Emotionally tough, but fucking fulfilling. And I loved working with so many strong female actresses. Ugh, Lorca's a genius. Okay. I'm going to start thinking about myself.

Claire exits.

(CONTINUED)

STILLS

Philip Seymour Hoffman as Caden Cotard

Samantha Morton as Hazel

Michelle Williams as Claire Keen

Catherine Keener as Adele Lack

Emily Watson as Tammy

Dianne Wiest as Ellen Bascomb/Millicent Weems

Jennifer Jason Leigh as Maria

Hope Davis as Madeline Gravis

Tom Noonan as Sammy Barnathan

Adele (Catherine Keener) trying to fix the broken faucet

Adele at work on a miniature in her painting studio, with Olive (Sadie Goldstein) in the background

Olive, Adele, and Caden (Philip Seymour Hoffman) at the breakfast table

Caden and Maria (Jennifer Jason Leigh) at an outdoor café in Berlin, Germany, before their fight

Madeline (Hope Davis) recommending *Little Winky* by Horace Azpiazu to Caden during a therapy session

Caden encountering Madeline on the plane to Germany

Hazel (Samantha Morton) preparing a drink for Caden

Claire (Michelle Williams) and Caden on a downtown Schenectady street

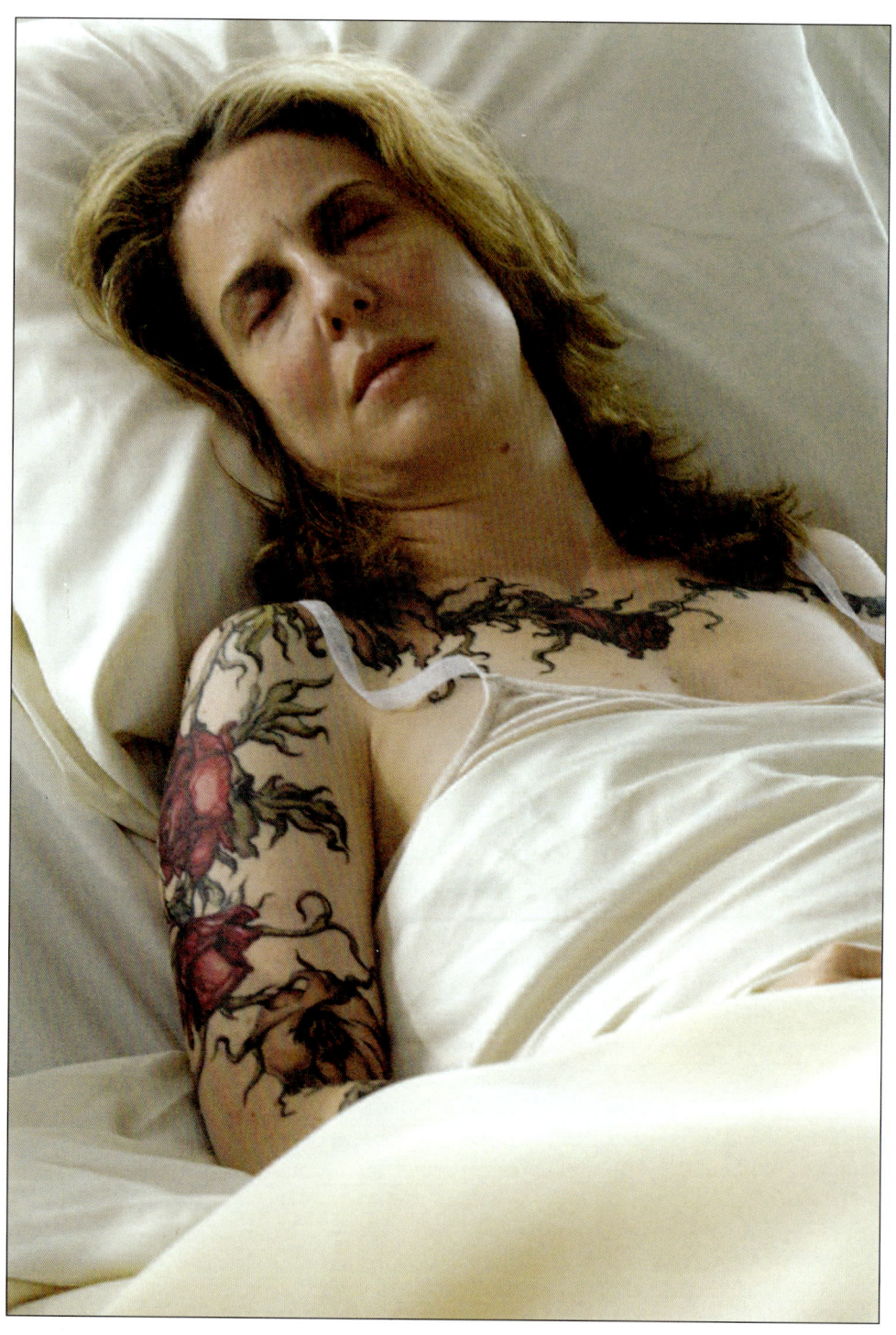

Adult Olive (Robin Weigert) dying of tattoo infections

Sammy (Tom Noonan) with Ariel (Daisy Tahan)

Caden, Claire, and Sammy on the fire escape

Caden and Hazel following Sammy to the warehouse within the warehouse (special effects not yet added)

Preparing a scene with Hazel's burning house set, with Tammy (Emily Watson) on the left

Caden and Hazel (special effects not yet added)

Tammy, Hazel, Caden, and Sammy at the director's table inside the warehouse within the warehouse (special effects not yet added)

Caden at a store, checking a wig called "The Director"

Tammy, Millicent (Dianne Wiest), and Caden, wearing "The Director" wig, at the director's table

Claire and Sammy on set in the warehouse in Claire's apartment (special effects not yet added)

Claire and Sammy on the apartment set

Charlie Kaufman on set under construction

Sammy about to jump, with stunt wire

Caden cleaning Adele's apartment

A much older Caden sitting on the stoop of Claire's apartment building

Sets inside the warehouse

119   CONTINUED:

                    SAMMY
               Start, huh?

Caden chuckles.

                    SAMMY (CONT'D)
                    (beat)
               Why did we leave Adele, Caden?

                    CADEN
               She left us. You know that better
               than anyone. Except me.

                    SAMMY
               Amazing artist though. The best
               living artist. There's no one who
               stares the truth in the face like
               she does. A sweet pussy, too.

Caden looks at Sammy, confused.

                    CADEN
               How do you know that?

                    SAMMY
               Oh. I read it.

                    CADEN
               Anyway, I don't know where she is.

A strange dirigible flies very low overhead.

                    SAMMY
               Maybe she's got a sublet in New
               York. Maybe the Met's doing a
               retrospective. Maybe, baby.

He hands Caden a slip of paper.

                    CADEN
               Why are you giving this to me?

                    SAMMY
               I want to follow you there and see
               how you lose even more of yourself.
               Research. For the part. Partner.

120   EXT. CITY STREET (NEAR 31Y BUILDING) - FALL 2026 - NIGHT   120

Dark, deserted part of town. The wind blows wet leaves. A
kid walks by in a Hallowe'en costume, looking lost.

                                                    (CONTINUED)

120   CONTINUED: 120

Caden finds the address: an old, narrow, very tall, very dark building. There's a piece of looseleaf paper with the handwritten note "Death in family. God relieve our grief." taped to the front door. He approaches the tenant buzzers and buzzes 31Y. The name on the apartment is Capgras. The door buzzes.

121   OMITTED   121*

122   INT. ELEVATOR (31Y BUILDING) - 2026 - MOMENTS LATER   122*

It's small. The walls are panelled with ancient, scarred wood. Caden presses "31." The doors close; the elevator ascends, swaying and creaking. The doors open on 17; nobody gets on. As they begin to close:

                    FAINT FARAWAY VOICE
               Hold it. Hold it, please.

Caden reaches for the "door open" button but doesn't press it. The doors close and the elevator continues its shaky ascent. The doors open on 31 and Caden exits.

123   INT. 31ST FLOOR HALLWAY (31Y BUILDING) - 2026 - CONTINUOUS   123

Sound of the elevator descending. Caden heads down the long hall, looking at apartment numbers. He gets to the end and is only at 31J. He turns and heads back. The elevator is ascending again. As he passes the elevator door, it opens and a very old, feeble-looking man or woman steps out.

                    OLD PERSON
               I asked you to hold the door.

          CADEN   OLD PERSON
    I'm sorry. I pressed it, but   You didn't press it.
    I think it was too late.

Caden continues to walk down the hall. The old person walks behind him. Caden looks behind him and smiles awkwardly.

                    CADEN
               Have a good night.

He picks up his pace, trying to be casual about it. He arrives at 31Y, glances over and sees the old person knocking feebly on a door down the hall.

                    OLD PERSON
               Frances, I need to go to the
               clinic. Something's terribly wrong
               with my nose.

                                                        (CONTINUED)

123   CONTINUED: 123

Caden knocks on 31Y. No answer. He knocks again. Down the hall, the door opens and another old person steps out into the hall. This person examines the first old person's nose.

                    OLD PERSON #2
          Oh yes. I see.

Old Person #2 squints over at Caden.

                    OLD PERSON #2 (CONT'D)
          Are you Ellen? Ellen?!

                    CADEN
          What?

                    OLD PERSON #2
                (approaching)
          Are you Ellen Bascomb? I'm to give
          the key to 31Y to Ellen Bascomb.

                    CADEN
                (beat)
          Yes, I'm Ellen.

Old Person #2 fishes a key out of the overcoat pocket.

                    OLD PERSON #2
          She said you should just go in and
          get started. She said, don't
          forget to change the sheets.

                    CADEN
          Ok. Thank you.

Old Person #2 turns and heads back down the hall to Old Person #1, whose nose has started to bleed.

                    OLD PERSON #2
          Oh dear.

Caden enters the apartment.

124   INT. 31Y - 2026 - CONTINUOUS   124

An expansive, well-decorated place. Someone was just here: there's a steaming cup of coffee on the kitchen table.

125   INT. 31Y BEDROOM - 2026 - MOMENTS LATER   125

Clothing strewn about. There's a handwritten note on the night table. He reads it:

                                                          (CONTINUED)

125 CONTINUED:

                    ADELE'S VOICE
          Hi Ellen. Be a doll and do the
          sheets and whatever is in the
          hamper. Your money is under the
          toaster. Kisses, Adele. ps. bag
          of stuff in bedroom closet for
          Goodwill. Take what you want.

126 INT. 31Y BATHROOM - 2026 - LATER

Caden scrubs the filthy toilet bowl.

127 INT. 31Y BEDROOM - 2026 - DAWN

Caden folds laundry and puts it away. He spots the bag of clothing and goes through it. There are several blouses and skirts, a red beret, and some lingerie.

128 EXT. 31Y APARTMENT BUILDING - 2026 - MORNING

Caden exits with bag of clothing. Several Latina and Eastern European cleaning ladies are exiting buildings also.

129 INT. CLAIRE APARTMENT (NYC APARTMENT) - 2026 - LATER

Caden enters. Claire is in her bathrobe, worried and angry.

                    CADEN
          I went for a walk. I had to think.

                    CLAIRE
          All night? You smell weird. Are
          you wearing lipstick?

                    CADEN
          No! What do I smell like? Like
          bad? Like an old person?

                    CLAIRE
          I don't know. Like mold? I don't
          know. Like mold and ... cleaning
          products? Like you're
          menstruating? I don't know!

130 INT. CLAIRE'S BATHROOM (NYC APARTMENT) - 2026 - MORNING

Caden is scrubbing himself raw in the shower.

131 INT. WAREHOUSE - CITY SET - 2026 - DAY

The actors are in their "apartments" and rehearsal is in progress.

(CONTINUED)

CONTINUED:

Caden walks along the scaffolding followed by Hazel. He hands scraps of paper to each actor he passes, then turns his attention to Sammy and Claire. She's in her underwear and getting dressed. Sammy comes up behind her and rubs her ass.

CLAIRE
I don't like that guy you got to play you.

SAMMY
You don't like Sammy? Why? I think he's good.

CLAIRE
I think you need to fire him.

Caden hands her a scrap of paper.

CLAIRE (CONT'D)
(reading, then to Caden)
Oh, fuck you. I'm forty-five years old. I don't want to do this shit anymore.

SAMMY
I'm not firing him, Claire. He's the best thing in the show. Next to you.

CLAIRE
He's coming on to me. He's feeling my ass during rehearsal.

SAMMY
He's your husband.

Claire turns to the real Caden and screams.

CLAIRE
He's not my Godamn husband! You are! What is wrong with you?

The actor underneath them pounds on his ceiling.

CADEN
Good, Jimmy!

SAMMY
(to Claire)
It's for the play. We're getting at something real here.

CLAIRE (CONT'D)
Ugh! I'm going to rehearsal.

(CONTINUED)

131   CONTINUED: (2)   131

She grabs her coat, tosses the note into the trash, and storms out and down the stairs.

                    CADEN
          That's great, you guys.

Sammy sits at the table and starts to write on scraps of paper. Hazel hovers behind him, watching.

                    CADEN (CONT'D)
          Beautiful, Sammy.

Caden leaves the set and steps onto his platform.

                    SAMMY
          Caden, time out?

          CADEN   SAMMY
     What's up?   I feel we need a Hazel in
                                   here. There's a whole side
                                   of Caden I'm not able to
                                   explore without a Hazel.

Caden looks over at Hazel. Claire watches Caden from the street corner.

                    CADEN
          I guess, yeah.

Claire walks off in a huff.

                    HAZEL
          I get to be a character? Hooray!

132   INT. ELEVATOR (31Y BUILDING) - 2026 - NIGHT   132

Caden rides up. The elevator stops. Old Person #1 gets on with a big bloody bandage covering his nose.

                    OLD PERSON
          Hello, Ellen.

Caden nods. They continue the ride in silence.

133   INT. 31Y BEDROOM - 2026 - NIGHT   133

Caden looks at the unmade bed, an imprint of a female form in the sheets. He touches it. He gets a melancholy look on his face. He lies on his back in the form. He sees a note on the night table:

                                                        (CONTINUED)

133   CONTINUED: 133

                        ADELE'S VOICE
              Hi Ellen. Crackerjack job last
              night! Would you do sheets again?
              We had quite a fuck last night and
              it's musky and gross. Kisses, A.

    Caden smells the sheets, strips the bed.

A134   EXT. 31Y APARTMENT BUILDING - 2026 - MORNING   A134

    Caden, strapped to a high window outside of Adele's
    apartment, washes it.

134   INT. 31Y KITCHEN - 2026 - MORNING   134

    Caden sips coffee at the kitchen table. He's writing a note:

                        CADEN'S VOICE
              Hi Adele. Relined the cabinets.
              Just wanted to let you know I won a
              MacArthur Grant and I'm mounting a
              play, which I think is going to be
              pure and truthful. Best --

    Caden hesitates for a moment, then signs it "Ellen."

135   INT. WAREHOUSE - CLAIRE'S APARTMENT SET - 2026 - DAY   135

    Caden and Hazel watch as Claire waits in her bathrobe in the
    kitchen and Sammy enters the "apartment."

                        CLAIRE
              Caden, what are you doing at night?
              I have a right to fucking know.

                        SAMMY
              I've been going to Adele's place.
              And cleaning it.

    Long pause. Caden rubs his eyes.

                        CLAIRE
              Do you know what I've given up for
              you? For this. For you. For you.

              SAMMY   CLAIRE
    I'm sorry.   I -- I thought I wanted to be
                                   just a working stage actress.
                                   But, y'know, I'm watching all
                                   the young girls crowding me
                                   out and it's --

                                                        (CONTINUED)

There's a knock on the door. Sammy just stands there.

> CLAIRE (CONT'D)
> Get the door. Please. Just...

Sammy opens it. Tammy, playing Hazel, stands there.

> TAMMY
> Uh-oh. This looks serious. Am I interrupting?

> SAMMY
> What's going on, Hazel?

> TAMMY
> Just wanted to tell you the girl playing me is able to start today.

> SAMMY
> Oh, good. That's good.

> CLAIRE
> That's all we need around here, two Hazels.

> TAMMY (CONT'D)
> Okay. I'll take that as my cue.

Tammy closes the door and leaves.

> CLAIRE
> Maybe you can clean *her* toilet.

> SAMMY
> Maybe I will.

> CLAIRE
> It's over, Caden.

> SAMMY
> Claire, no.

> CLAIRE
> I'm not talking to you.

Claire turns to Caden.

> CADEN
> *I* didn't say I was going to clean Hazel's toilet. He did.

> CLAIRE
> But you thought it.

There's a silence. Hazel watches Caden closely.

(CONTINUED)

                        CADEN
            I thought it. But I didn't say it.

Claire packs up her stuff.

                        CLAIRE
            I got an offer to do Needleman in a
            Haystack and I'm going to take it.
            I want you out of the apartment.
            The real one. You can keep this
            one.

Claire heads down the stairs.

                        CADEN
            Jesus. Claire! Please!

                        HAZEL
            Already put out a call for a Claire
            replacement. Would you really
            clean my bathroom?

                        CADEN
                (beat, sadly)
            Yeah.

                        HAZEL
            God, Caden, it's all so fucked.

136   INT. WAREHOUSE - BATHROOM - 2026 - DAY   136

Caden digs in his bag, pulls out a sponge, gets on his hands and knees and scrubs the floor.

137   INT. METROPOLITAN MUSEUM OF ART - 2026 - DAY   137

Caden, wearing a pair of magnifying glasses that flip up and down, enters a crowded gallery of people wearing similar glasses. The paintings are microscopic. Museum visitors use the special glasses to study the paintings. There's a wall inscribed "Small Miracles: The Paintings of Adele Lack." Biographical info is under. Caden squeezes his way to the wall to look at paintings. He sees one of an African female genital mutilation ceremony; a woman weeping over the grave of a child; a man raping a woman. He comes to a wall titled: "Women I Love." He sees a self-portrait of Adele, a portrait of Maria, a portrait of Olive, naked and covered in tattoos. Then he comes to a portrait entitled "Ellen Bascomb." He steps back for a second, unable to look. The people behind him are impatient. Finally he flips the glasses and studies the painting. Ellen appears to be a chubby, 40 year old white woman, her mousy brown hair tied back in a kerchief.

                                                        (CONTINUED)

137 CONTINUED: 137

She is naked and spreading her vulva for the viewer. She has a kind face and what appears to be an appendectomy scar.

138 INT. CLAIRE'S KITCHEN (NYC APARTMENT) - 2026 - DAY   138

Caden moves boxes. Claire sits at the kitchen table with an actor. They are rehearsing lines from Needleman in a Haystack.

                    CADEN
This is the end of my stuff.

        CLAIRE   ACTOR
Bye.   Bye.

Caden heads out the apartment door.

139 INT. APARTMENT HALLWAY (CLAIRE'S NYC APT.) - 2026 - CONTINUOUS   139

Caden enters the apartment next door and closes the door.

140 INT. CADEN'S APARTMENT - 2026 - CONTINUOUS   140

It's filled with boxes. Caden hears laughter coming from next door. He puts his ear against the wall to listen.

141 EXT. CADEN'S APARTMENT BUILDING - 2026 - DAY   141

Caden exits, crosses the street, and looks up, trying to see in Claire's window. He sees her walk by, then nothing.

142 INT. WAREHOUSE - 2026 - DAY   142

Caden sits with Hazel at a table facing the giant, open apartment building structure. An actress plays Claire. She sits at the kitchen table of her apartment with an actor playing the actor. They both hold scripts and read from Needleman in a Haystack. Sammy is in front of the building, looking up. Caden looks troubled. Tammy sits to the side of Hazel and studies her. Every once in a while, Hazel self-consciously glances over at Tammy, who does not avert her gaze.

                    CADEN
This is a lie!

Caden paces. The actors stop what they're doing, sit with their legs dangling off the edge of their apartments, wait for instructions. Caden limps off to the set designer's office.

A143　INT. WAREHOUSE - WILL'S OFFICE - 2026 - CONTINUOUS　A143

Caden enters the office. Will, the production designer, looks up from his drafting table.

      CADEN
 Wall it up.

143　INT. WAREHOUSE - CITY SET - 2028 - DAY　143

Sammy stands across the street from the walled-up apartment building, an exact replica of the real one. He looks up at Claire's lighted window. Caden watches, pleased.

144　INT. CADEN'S APARTMENT - 2029 - NIGHT　144

Caden, hooked up to pumps, tries to sleep on the floor, surrounded by boxes. He listens to Claire having sex next door. He detaches his pumps, gets dressed.

145　INT. 31Y BEDROOM - 2029 - NIGHT　145

Caden sits on the bed and reads a note from Adele:

      ADELE'S VOICE
  Good for you with your grant!
  Listen, I fixed up the walk-in as a
  sort of bedroom if you want. We'd
  love to have you and you wouldn't
  have to schlep all the way to
  Queens. Just a thought. Kisses.
  A.

146　INT. 31Y WALK-IN CLOSET - 2029 - NIGHT　146

Caden sees an unmade cot in the corner and a few cardboard boxes marked "Stuff for Olive." The "Olive" is crossed out and replaced with "Caden."

147　INT. 31Y WALK-IN CLOSET - 2029 - LATER　147

The boxes are empty as Caden finishes making the bed. The room is decorated in a girly manner. Pink bedspread. Girly lamps and furniture. Girly prints on the walls.

148　EXT. CITY SET (INT. WAREHOUSE SET) - 2031 - DAY　148

Sammy, walking with a cane, exits his apartment building set and walks down the street. Caden and Hazel follow. Sammy passes people, nods hello to some. He stops at a newsstand and buys a paper. The set seems to go on forever.

A149   EXT. WAREHOUSE STREET (INT. WAREHOUSE SET) - 2031 -   A149
            CONTINUOUS

    Eventually Sammy arrives at a warehouse that looks exactly like the warehouse they are in. He enters.

149   EXT. CITY STREET (INT. WAREHOUSE-WITHIN-WAREHOUSE) - 2031 - 149
            CONTINUOUS

    Inside it looks exactly like the warehouse, including a duplicate city set. Sammy hands little scraps of paper to people, then dumps his pack on the table where Tammy sits. Hazel and Caden watch.

                    SAMMY
            Morning, Haze.

                    TAMMY
            Hi, Caden. How was your night?

                    SAMMY
            Okay. Yours?

                    TAMMY
            Eh. Philip was colicky. I was up
            all night.

    Caden looks over at Hazel for confirmation. She nods, slightly freaked out.

                    CADEN
            Sorry.

                    SAMMY
                (to Tammy)
            Sorry. Everybody here?

                    TAMMY
                (looking at clipboard)
            Sammy's not here. Jimmy called and
            said there's some subway problem.

    Jimmy rushes into the warehouse.

                    JIMMY
            Sorry. Sorry, sorry, sorry.
                (sweetly)
            Hi, Hazel.

                    TAMMY
            Hi, Sammy.

(CONTINUED)

149   CONTINUED: 149

>   SAMMY
>   (to Tammy)
>   Sammy likes you.

Caden looks at Hazel. She nods.

>   SAMMY (CONT'D)
>   Hazel, could you get everyone
>   situated? I need to speak to Will
>   about some new sets.

Sammy pulls some Polaroids out of his backpack.

>   TAMMY
>   Yeah. We'll take it from June 9th?

Sammy nods, heads toward the set designer's office.

>   CADEN
>   Oh, shit. I need to do that, too.
>   Haze, keep an eye on things?

>   HAZEL
>   Yup. June 9th?

Caden nods, rushes out the door of the warehouse set.

150   OMITTED   150*

A151   EXT. UNFINISHED BRICK BUILDING (BROOKLYN BRIDGE PARK)(INT.   A151*
       WAREHOUSE) - 2031 - CONTINUOUS

Caden finds Will up on some scaffolding, working on the set.

>   CADEN
>   Will, I need you to build this.

Caden hands Will shots of the exterior and interiors of Adele's building and of apartment 31Y.

151   INT. WAREHOUSE - AUDITION CORNER - 2031 - LATER   151

Caden sits at his desk. There are several overweight women waiting on the other side of the partition. Hazel ushers one in. She's a ringer for the painting of Ellen.

>   CADEN
>   Hazel, what do you think of this
>   title: <u>Unknown, Unkissed, and Lost</u>?

>   HAZEL
>   Eh. Caden this is Millicent Weems.

(CONTINUED)

151   CONTINUED: 151

                         CADEN
               Hi, Millicent. Have a seat. How
               are you at cleaning?

                         MILLICENT
                    (sitting)
               I'm very, very good at it.

                         CADEN
               Because this part requires a lot of
               it. You'd play a cleaning lady.

                         MILLICENT
               I played Egga the cleaning lady in
               Hedda Gabler at the Roundabout.

                    CADEN   MILLICENT
     Great. Okay.   And Mrs. Dobson in Scrub-a-
                                          Dub at the Pantages.

                         CADEN
               You're weirdly close to what I've
               visualized for this character.

                         MILLICENT
               Glad to be weirdly close.

     Millicent and Caden study each other.

152   EXT. CITY STREETS (INT. WAREHOUSE SET) - 2032 - DAY   152

     Caden heads to the warehouse set. He hands paper scraps to
     shopkeepers, pedestrians, a guy sweeping the street.

                         CADEN
               Good work, everyone.

     Nobody acknowledges him.

A153   INT. WAREHOUSE - WAREHOUSE SET - 2032 - CONTINUOUS   A153

     Caden enters the warehouse set. Tammy sits alone at the card
     table. There's activity on the street and movement can be
     seen in various windows.

                         CADEN
               Where're Sammy and Hazel?

     Tammy jerks her head to the left. Caden sees that Sammy has
     Hazel with her back against a wall. They are talking
     intimately. Caden approaches.

                                                           (CONTINUED)

CADEN (CONT'D)
Hey, Sammy, what are you doing?

Sammy and Hazel look over casually.

SAMMY
Hi, Caden. I'm being you. You like Hazel; I like Hazel.

CADEN
This Hazel doesn't exist for you. If you want to like a Hazel, like that one.

Caden points indicates Tammy. Sammy squints over.

TAMMY
That's what I tried to tell him!

HAZEL
Aw, no harm, no foul, Caden. It's Equity break anyway.
(loud)
Ten minutes, everybody!

The actors playing the people on the street immediately stop what they're doing. Actors pour from apartment buildings and shops, lighting cigarettes and talking on cell phones. Sammy goes off.

CADEN
Hazel.

HAZEL
What?

CADEN (CONT'D)
You don't like him, do you?

HAZEL
Kind of. He reminds me of you.

CADEN
I'm me. You don't need someone to remind you of me.

HAZEL
Don't worry, Caden. I like you more. I do. Sammy's just fun.

CADEN
I'm fun.

HAZEL
Oh, sweetie. No, you're not.

Caden's cell phone rings. He answers it.

(CONTINUED)

A153   CONTINUED: (2)   A153

                    CADEN   VOICE
          Yes?   Is this Caden Cotard?

                    CADEN   VOICE
          Yes.   This is Officer Mark Mellman
                                        of Schnectady P.D.

                    CADEN   VOICE
          Yes?   I'm sorry to inform you, your
                                        mother has been the victim of
                                        a home invasion.

153   EXT. CEMETERY - 2032 - DAY   153

       A funeral is in progress. Caden stands with Tammy and his
       father as his mother's coffin is lowered into the ground.
       The coffin is banged up and crumbling.

154   INT. CADEN'S MOTHER'S HOUSE - 2032 - DAY   154

       Lots of mourners. Caden sits on the couch with Tammy.

                         CADEN
               Was my father standing with us?

                         TAMMY
               I don't know what he looks like.

                         CADEN
               He's dead. He looks dead, I guess.

                         TAMMY
               Probably wasn't him then.

                         CADEN
               A little moustache?

       She shrugs.

                         CADE
               Anyway, Thanks for coming with me.

                         TAMMY
               It's okay.

                         CADEN
               I asked Hazel but she was busy
               tonight and you're the next best
               thing. I mean, it isn't that
               you're the next best thing but
               because you play her, it feels
               comforting. Does that make sense?
                         (MORE)

                                                              (CONTINUED)

154   CONTINUED: 154

                    CADEN (CONT'D)
          Although the thing is offstage
          you're nothing like her. You play
          her very well though. Did Hazel
          mention what she was doing tonight
          because I called her house before
          we left and her husband said she
          wasn't going to be back till late
          and I thought that was weird
          because she told me Philip was
          sick.

                    TAMMY
          She's going to dinner with Sammy.

                    CADEN
              (calmly)
          That's interesting.

          TAMMY   CADEN
He's supposed to like *me*.   I'll have another talk with
                              him. Can you excuse me. I
                              need to use the bathroom.

Caden gets up and turns to leave.

                    TAMMY
          Don't forget your phone.

                    CADEN
          Thank you, Yammy.

Caden takes the phone and limps off.

155   EXT. CADEN'S MOTHER'S BACK DECK - 2032 - DAY   155

Caden talks on his cell.

                    CADEN
          Hey. What you up to?

                                              INTERCUT WITH:

A156 INT. HAZEL'S CAR - 2032 - SAME   A156

Hazel's driving while talking on her cell.

                    HAZEL'S VOICE
          In my car. Heading to dinner with
          Sammy.

                    CADEN
          Why didn't you tell me that before?

                                                           (CONTINUED)

A156 CONTINUED: A156

                         HAZEL
               Caden. I don't want to say things
               that are going to make you sad.

                         CADEN
               It mostly makes me sad that it
               doesn't make you sad.

                         HAZEL
               You want me to be sad that
               someone's taking me out to dinner?
               I don't know how to do that.

                         CADEN
               I want you to be sad that we had
               something really special and it's
               going away!

                         HAZEL
               It just happened, Caden. I didn't
               plan it. You were with Claire.
               This probably isn't going to go
               anywhere, sweetie. I'm still your
               girl.

          CADEN   HAZEL'S VOICE
Oh, Haze. C'mon.   It's just dinner. He's got
                              stories! It just seems fun.

                         CADEN
               He has stories about me!

                         HAZEL
               Caden, I know everything about you
               and it's all adorable. I love you
               and I always will. So don't worry.
               I gotta go, I'm there.

     Hazel hangs up. Caden stands there for a minute.

156 INT. CADEN'S MOTHER'S KITCHEN - 2032 - NIGHT   156

     The house has emptied out. Caden and Tammy straighten.

                         CADEN
               Did you always want to be an
               actress?

                         TAMMY
               Every girl wants to be an actress.

                                                              (CONTINUED)

156   CONTINUED: 156

                        CADEN
              Is that true?

                        TAMMY
              I did. So I figure everyone does.

157   INT. CADEN'S MOTHER'S BEDROOM - 2032 - LATER   157

       Looks like there's been a horrible struggle. The bed is
       covered with blood. Caden and Tammy stare at it.

                        CADEN
              I thought someone would've cleaned
              it up.

                        TAMMY
              Who?

                        CADEN
              I don't know! Someone.

158   INT. CADEN'S CHILDHOOD ROOM - 2032 - LATER   158

       It's a kid's room. Caden and Tammy stand there.

                        CADEN
              This is my room. You can sleep
              here.

                        TAMMY
              Where will you sleep?

                        CADEN
              The living room couch.

                        TAMMY
              Don't you want to sleep with me?

              CADEN   TAMMY
       Um...   It's just sex.

                        CADEN
              Okay. If you think it's okay.

       Tammy laughs, matter-of-factly gets undressed in front of
       Caden. He just stands there uncomfortably.

                        CADEN (CONT'D)
              How can you be like that?

                        TAMMY
              I get undressed every day.

                                                              (CONTINUED)

CADEN
In front of someone is different.

TAMMY
I don't see why.

CADEN
Maybe because you have a beautiful body. Maybe that makes it easier.

TAMMY
I suppose it might. Do you want to fuck?

CADEN
I do. Yes. Um. Do you?

TAMMY
It'd be fine.

Caden starts to cry.

CADEN
I'm sorry. I'm very lonely. I don't know what's wrong. I just -- I'm sorry. Can you understand? Do you understand loneliness?

TAMMY
Yeah, I mean, I don't know. I feel okay mostly. Fucking might help.

CADEN
I'm sorry.

TAMMY
It's okay. I don't mind. Take your clothes off.

CADEN
You're very pretty.

TAMMY
Thanks.

CADEN
Sometimes I wish I were pretty like that.

TAMMY
You wish you were a chick?

(CONTINUED)

                                CADEN
                          (long pause)
                    Sometimes I think I might've been
                    better at it.

                                TAMMY
                    Interesting. It's kind of a drag
                    in a lot of ways. You like guys?

                                CADEN
                    No. No. I like women. I only
                    like women.

                                TAMMY
                    Well, I'm getting cold.

She climbs into bed.

                                TAMMY (CONT'D)
                    Take off your clothes.

Caden does, awkwardly and shyly. He then stands there naked.
Tammy smiles sweetly at him.

                                TAMMY (CONT'D)
                    Pretty Caden.

                                CADEN
                    Thanks. Thank you for saying that.

                                TAMMY
                    Come to bed, Pretty Caden.

Caden turns off the lights and climbs into the twin bed with
Tammy. She looks at his face, then kisses him.

159   INT. CADEN'S CAR - 2032 - MORNING   159

A residential street in Schenectady. Caden drives and Tammy
sits in the front passenger seat.

                                TAMMY
                    What is attractive? How are
                    attractive people treated, how do
                    they feel? How do unattractive
                    people feel, how are they treated?
                    How do attractive people feel about
                    unattractive people, how do
                    unattractive people feel about
                    attractive people? How do
                    unattractive people feel about
                    other unattractive people?
                              (MORE)

                                                          (CONTINUED)

159   CONTINUED: 159

                    TAMMY (CONT'D)
            How do attractive people feel about
            other attractive people? How do
            unattractive men feel about
            unattractive women? How do
            unattractive men feel about
            attractive women? How do
            attractive men feel about
            unattractive women? How do
            attractive women feel about
            unattractive men? How do old
            people feel about attractive
            people? How do attractive people
            feel about old people? This is my
            study.

Caden slows down.

                    CADEN
            That's Hazel's house.

Caden points to the house with smoke seeping out the windows.

                    TAMMY
            Huh. Do you think we should have a
            Hazel's house on the set for me?

                    CADEN
            Um...

                    TAMMY
            It would be verisimilitudinous.

                    CADEN
            Yeah. I don't know. I have to
            speak to the fire marshal.

                    TAMMY
            It would be very verisimilitudinous
            if you could.

160   EXT. HIGHWAY (INT. WAREHOUSE) - 2032 - DAY   160

Hazel drives a golf cart along a fake highway. Caden and
Tammy sit in back. Hazel eyes them in the rearview mirror.
They seem cozy. Hazel scowls. Technicians are on the side
of the road putting in plants and trees.

                    CADEN
            I think both of you Hazels are
            going to like this. Turn off here.

Hazel rolls her eyes, drives down an exit ramp.

161   EXT. BURNING HOUSE STREET (INT. WAREHOUSE SET) - 2032 - DAY   161

Hazel drives the golf cart down the street in a state of near completion. She stops in front of a replica of her house.

> CADEN
> Hank! Okay!

The house begins to smoke.

> TAMMY
> My house!

Tammy kisses Caden on the cheek and runs into the house.

> HAZEL
> Is there no end to your pussy kissing?

> CADEN
> It's verisimilitudinous. I'm thinking of that as a title.

> HAZEL
> Whatever. I've got work to do. Tell your girlfriend to get out here if she wants a ride back.

> CADEN
> She's not my girlfriend.

> HAZEL
> Give it a rest, Caden. I can smell her on your breath.

> CADEN
> (beat)
> Tammy! We have to get back.

162   INT. APARTMENT HALLWAY (INT. WAREHOUSE SET) - 2032 - DAY   162

Sammy walks down the hall followed by Tammy. He stops at various doorways and listens to conversations or other noises within the apartments. They are followed by Caden and Hazel.

> SAMMY
> Jeremy is playing to us. Tell him he simply needs to talk to Donna. We'll hear what we hear.

Tammy takes down the note.

(CONTINUED)

CONTINUED:

          CADEN
Sammy's explaining too much. Feels expository. Needs to be shorthand, like, "Jeremy big."

Hazel writes that down. They all continue down the hall.

          TAMMY
Caden? Can we stop for a second?

          CADEN
Sure.

          TAMMY
If Hazel's in love with Sammy and Caden's in love with Hazel, there would be a dramatic confrontation, where Caden turns to me and says, "It's obvious he's a substitute for me." I think then Hazel could have a good moment where she cries or gets angry. I'm not sure which yet, but it feels dramatically sound.

          HAZEL
That didn't happen, Caden.

          TAMMY
I think Hazel would do that, Hazel.

          HAZEL
But Hazel hasn't done it, Tammy.

     TAMMY   CADEN
Caden? What do you think?   I think we could try it.

     TAMMY   HAZEL
Great!   Fuck. I'm going out for a smoke.

They watch her go. Caden turns back to the others.

          CADEN
Let's try it. Maybe it could happen at the director's table.

EXT. CITY STREET (INT. WAREHOUSE SET) - 2032 - DAY

Caden and Hazel sit at the director's table. The street life of the play is going on around them.

(CONTINUED)

CADEN
Tammy was right. I don't understand why you're with Sammy.

HAZEL
He's nice. He's available. He fucks me without crying.

CADEN
That happened one time! You *fucked* him?

HAZEL
Yes! And you and I *only* fucked one time that's why you only *cried* one time! I give you endless opportunities.

CADEN
What do you mean, he's available? Since when are you available?

HAZEL
Derek left. Because of you!

CADEN
When? How come you never told me?

HAZEL
I don't know, Caden. How come a lot of things? It's not like we can start fresh, like Sammy and I can. There's all this pressure on us. We're finally both free and there's all this fucking pressure.

CADEN
Fuck. I have to let the actor who plays Derek go. What is his name?

HAZEL
That's such a romantic response. I'm touched.

CADEN
It's not my response. It just crossed my mind. We have enormous budgetary concerns here.

(CONTINUED)

HAZEL
Ugh. Forget it.
        (looking in book)
Derek is played by Joe --

CADEN
Stop, okay. Just stop.

HAZEL
I don't like Tammy and she's nothing like me. How can you like her? Joe Abernathy.

CADEN
She looks like you. And --

HAZEL
No she does not.

CADEN
-- and she offered to have sex with me. Abernathy?

HAZEL
Yes. Was it good?

CADEN
I don't know. Yeah. It was nice.

HAZEL
Ugh.

CADEN
I'm just trying to be honest. It was nice. Not earth-shattering.

HAZEL
Did you cry?

CADEN
No!

HAZEL
You're making progress.

CADEN
Okay, I cried a little before.
        (long pause)
Hazel, you've been part of me forever. Don't you know that? I breathe your name in every exhalation.

HAZEL
        (stops)
Oh, Caden. Oh, fuck. What the fuck are we doing?

CADEN
I don't know.

(CONTINUED)

163   CONTINUED: (3)   163

Hazel latches her pinky around Caden's. Sammy has been watching the whole thing from behind a pillar. Caden glances at his watch.

                    CADEN (CONT'D)
          Crap, Ellen's October 23rd scene!

164   INT. ELEVATOR (31Y BUILDING) (INT. WAREHOUSE SET) - 2032 -   164
        DAY   *

Millicent, Hazel, and Caden wait in the elevator. The elevator begins to ascend. Instead of a motor, the sound of grunting men is heard. The elevator stops short and sways a little bit.

                    WORKER (O.S.)
          Sorry, everybody!

Caden pulls off a wall panel, and sticks his head through.

A165   INT. ELEVATOR SHAFT (31Y BUILDING) (INT. WAREHOUSE SET) -   A165
        2032 - SAME

Caden looks down the shaft. Five guys hold the elevator with a rope and pulley system.

                    CADEN
          What's going on, Maurice?

                    MAURICE
          Sorry. We have a couple of new guys
          on and we're not in sync yet.

                    CADEN
          Okay. Are we good to go?

                    MAURICE
          Yup.

B165   INT. ELEVATOR (31Y BUILDING) (INT. WAREHOUSE SET) - 2032 -   B165
        SAME   *

Caden replaces the panel. The elevator continues its ascent to the sound of grunting men. It stops. The doors open and Old Person (actor version) with bandaged nose gets on.

                    OLD PERSON
          Hi, Ellen.

                    MILLICENT
          Hello.

                                                          (CONTINUED)

B165 CONTINUED: B165

>   The doors close. The elevator ascends to the 31st floor.
>   The doors open and Millicent, Old Person, Caden, and Hazel
>   exit.

C165 INT. 31ST FLOOR HALLWAY (31Y BUILDING) (INT. WAREHOUSE SET) C165
      - 2032 - CONTINUOUS

>   The elevator doors close. Millicent, Old Person, Caden, and
>   Hazel walk down the hall. Old Person knocks on a door and is
>   admitted by Old Person #2 (actor version). Millicent lets
>   herself in to 31Y, closes the door. Caden and Hazel stand
>   outside and listen. Silence for a while, then a vacuum
>   cleaner. The vacuum cleaner turns off.

>   MILLICENT (O.S.)
>   Oh, Hi, Adele!

>   ADELE (O.S.)
>   Hi, Ellen. How are you tonight?

>   Caden turns to Hazel.

>   CADEN
>   Did we hire an Adele?

>   Hazel shakes her head no.

ADELE (O.S.)	MILLICENT (O.S.)
That's one of my blouses?	Yes. I love it. Thank you so much.

>   ADELE (O.S.)
>   Good. Would you be a doll and
>   handwash some of my delicates?

MILLICENT (O.S.)	CADEN
Of course.	You have the master?

>   Hazel hands him a key. Caden opens the door.

165 INT. 31Y (INT. WAREHOUSE SET) - 2032 - DAY   165 *

>   Caden finds Millicent vacuuming the living room.

>   MILLICENT
>   (surprised)
>   Are we breaking?

>   She turns off the vacuum cleaner.

>   CADEN
>   You were just talking to Adele.

(CONTINUED)

165   CONTINUED: 165

                    MILLICENT
                 (perplexed)
            Adele? No. Just cleaning.

Caden stares at Millicent, then tears through the apartment, looking in every room. Nobody there. He finds a sink full of panties soaking in detergent.

166   EXT. HOTEL STREET (INT. WAREHOUSE SET) - 2032 - NIGHT   166

Caden and Hazel walk past the set of the hotel she had stayed at with her family.

                    CADEN
            Look familiar?

                    HAZEL
            Oh, is this the place I stayed with
            Derek and the kids? We had so much
            fun that trip.

Caden looks crestfallen. There's a commotion. The actors on the street all look up. Caden and Hazel join them. Sammy stands on the ledge of a hig window.

                    HAZEL (CONT'D)
            Oh fuck. Caden.

                    CADEN
            That's where I was going to jump
            from! No fair, Sammy!

                    HAZEL
                 (screaming)
            Sammy! Sammy! Just stay right
            where you are! I'm coming up!

Hazel rushes into the building set.

                    SAMMY
            There's nothing to talk about,
            Hazel! This is not your fault!

                    CADEN
            You can't do this! You can't jump
            from where I was going to jump
            from!

                    SAMMY
            After me, there's no one left to
            watch you. You'll see.
                 (MORE)

                                                        (CONTINUED)

166   CONTINUED: 166

                    SAMMY (CONT'D)
          You'll wither anonymously in a hell
          of lack of interest.

                    CADEN
          What?! What does that even mean?
          I don't understand what the fuck
          anyone's talking about!

                    SAMMY
          Yeah, well, you stole your girl
          from me! And now I have nothing
          now!

     Sammy leaps. The actors below scatter. Sammy hits hard,
     breaks through the fake cement, and is dead. Blood
     everywhere. Hazel appears in a window on the 10th floor.

167 EXT. NYC CEMETERY - 2032 - DAY 167

     Sammy is buried. An enormous crowd there: all the actors
     from the play, Caden and Hazel in front. Hazel weeps. Caden
     looks at the assembled group, from face to face.

                    CADEN
          I know how to do it now. There are
          nearly *thirteen million* people in
          the world. Try to imagine that many
          people! None of those people is an
          extra. They're all the leads of
          their own stories. They have to be
          given their due.

168 INT. WAREHOUSE - CEMETERY SET - 2035 - DAY 168

     The actor playing Sammy is in the coffin. There's an
     enormous crowd. Tammy plays Hazel and weeps. A stand-in for
     Sammy as Caden stands next to her. Caden and Hazel watch
     from the director's table.

                    CADEN
          Do you see what I'm saying?

     Hazel has her head in her hands. She looks over at Caden,
     imploringly.

                    HAZEL
          Come over tonight? Please?

169 OMITTED 169

170   INT. BURNING HOUSE - BEDROOM - 2035 - NIGHT   170

The smoke is thick and there are flames. Hazel, in a robe, walks around lighting candles. Caden unpacks his pumps and monitors and places them next to the bed.

                    CADEN
        We could get a place together. We
        could get a loft.

                    HAZEL
        God, Caden, that sounds nice. I
        miss my daughter. Maybe she could
        come live with us.

                    CADEN
        Yeah. I miss Olive. And the other
        one. The retarded one.

                    HAZEL
        I'm a bad person.

CADEN	HAZEL
No you're not. I'm a bad person.	I am. I should never... have gone out with Sammy. I was just trying to get to you.

                    CADEN
        You can't cause someone to kill
        himself. He was troubled.

                    HAZEL
        I'm so ashamed of myself.

Caden walks over to her and touches her shoulder.

                    HAZEL (CONT'D)
        Oh, Caden. I wish we had this when
        we were young. And all the years
        in between. So many years, so
        fast.
            (crying)
        What did we do?

Caden kisses Hazel's forehead. She coughs and smiles up at him, then cranes her neck and kisses him on the lips.

                    CADEN
        My heart aches so much for you.

(CONTINUED)

                    HAZEL
          We're here, Caden. I'm here.

                    CADEN
          I'm aching for it being over.

                    HAZEL
          Yeah. The end is built in to the
          beginning. What can you do?

                    CADEN
          God. You're just perfect.

                    HAZEL
          I'm a mess. But we fit, don't we.

They kiss, then Hazel climbs into bed.

                    CADEN
          It doesn't always happen for me
          now. Because of the medication and
          everything. I take a lot of pills.

                    HAZEL
          I don't care. It's okay.

                    CADEN
               (climbing into bed)
          I'm embarrassed. I just want you
          to know it's not you. And it's not
          me. It's the medication.

They are tender and quiet and intensely focused. The smoke in the room is dense. When it's over, they lie there quietly, with the occasional cough from both of them. Caden cries quietly.

                    CADEN (CONT'D)
          I'm sorry.

                    HAZEL
          It's okay. It's different crying
          this time. I can tell. I'm
          crying, too. And I cried last
          time. After you left. I never
          told you. But I cried, too.

Caden kisses her again.

                    CADEN
          I have a title. The Obscure Moon
          Lighting an Obscure World.

                                              (CONTINUED)

                    HAZEL
          I think it might be too much.

171   INT. BURNING HOUSE - KITCHEN - 2035 - MORNING

Caden agitatedly paces through the dense smoke. He passes a scrapbook on the table. It's open to a page with ripped-up napkin pieces glued to it. He's crying hard. There's mumbling, quiet conversation coming from somewhere. He walks into --

172   INT. BURNING HOUSE - BEDROOM - 2035 - CONTINUOUS

Hazel lies in bed. A medic hovers over her, swabs in her mouth and pulls out cotton black with soot.

                    MEDIC
          Might be smoke inhalation.

Caden just nods his head for a long time.

173   INT. CADEN'S CAR - 2041 - DAY

Caden drives. He stops at a school crossing as a group of young children are led across the street in front of his car. A young girl with red hair is among them. She looks at Caden and he is struck by her resemblance to young Olive. Suddenly the passenger door opens and Maria gets in the car. He glances over at her, then looks back out the windshield.

                    MARIA
          Olive wants to see you. God knows
          why; the way you abandoned her.

          CADEN   MARIA
     Oh, shut up.   She's had a fucked-up life
                                with issues, thanks to you.

          CADEN   MARIA
     You're insane.   She's dying, asshole. Is
                                that insane enough for you?

                    MARIA (CONT'D)
          Anyway, she wants to say goodbye to
          you. God knows the fuck why.

174   INT. NYC HOSPITAL ROOM - 2041 - DAY

Maria leads Caden into the room. Olive, 40, lies in bed, emaciated and pale. Maria and Olive speak only in German.

                                                    (CONTINUED)

                    MARIA   OLIVE
          Hello, darling.   Hi.

                    MARIA
          This is him.

                    OLIVE   CADEN
          Hello.   Hi, Olive.   I've missed you
                                    so much.

                    OLIVE
          Maria, would you leave us?

Maria kisses Olive again on the forehead.

                    MARIA
          In heaven, my darling.

Maria exits.

                    OLIVE
               (broken English)
          Forgive me but no longer remember
          English. Speak German?

                    CADEN   OLIVE
          No. I'm sorry.   I had hope you have learned.

Weakly, Olive points to a headset on her night table. She
pantomimes putting it on. Caden puts it on. Olive puts on
her own. There follows a slightly delayed and staticky
translation, in an accented male voice, of everything Olive
says, with a delay between what Caden says and Olive's
response, as she listens in translation.

                    OLIVE (CONT'D)
          I'm dying, as I'm sure Maria told
          you. The flower tattoos have
          become infected and they're dying.
          So I am, as well. This is life.

Olive pulls down her hospital gown a bit to show Caden the
now sickly and decayed flower tattoos.

                    CADEN
          It's Maria. She did this.

                    OLIVE
          Maria gave me reason to live once
          you left. The flowers defined me.

                                                      (CONTINUED)

CADEN
Your mother and Maria took you away. I tried for years to find you. I didn't leave you.

OLIVE
You did *something*.

Caden is affected by this. It resonates.

OLIVE (CONT'D)
I want to talk to you about your homosexuality.

CADEN
What? I'm not a homosexual!

OLIVE
Maria said you would deny it.

CADEN
She's lying to you.

OLIVE
I had the same struggle when I first fell in love with Maria and we began to have dirty, aching sex.

CADEN
Maria is your lover?

OLIVE
Of course. She introduced me to myself. To my vagina and to hers.

CADEN
You have no idea how evil she is.

OLIVE
I need to forgive you before I die, but I can't forgive someone who has not asked for forgiveness.

CADEN
I --

OLIVE
I have no time! I need you to ask for forgiveness!

(CONTINUED)

                    CADEN
              (long pause)
         Can you ever forgive me?

                    OLIVE
         For what?

                    CADEN
         For abandoning you.

                    OLIVE
         "For abandoning you to have anal
         sex with my homosexual lover Eric."

                    CADEN
         For abandoning you to be have anal
         sex with my homosexual lover Eric.

                    OLIVE
              (long hesitation)
         No. No, I'm sorry, I cannot.

    Olive dies. Dead flower petals slip from her hospital gown.
    Caden sits there. Maria hurries rushes to Olive's side.

                    MARIA
         I hope you're happy, faggot.

    Caden gets up and leaves.

175   EXT. NYC STREET - SUMMER 2045 - DAY   175

    It's sweltering. Caden sits on his stoop, holding some dead
    flower petals, watching the world pass by. People are sick,
    angry. Some people wear gas masks. Government vehicles with
    strange symbols and gun turrets drive by. A woman walks a
    naked man on a leash. He defecates on the sidewalk. A wild-
    eyed man in a white t-shirt and Santa hat attacks Caden. As
    he knocks Caden to the ground and wrestles with him, Caden
    sees the t-shirt has a little dot: a painting from Adele's
    show. It's a moment in time, a street scene very much like
    the one Caden's in. In the painting, a man in a white t-
    shirt and Santa hat beats up a man who looks like Caden. The
    flower petals blow away. Caden tries to limp after them.

176   EXT. NYC STREET - 2045 - NIGHT   176

    Caden dials his cell phone.

                    HAZEL'S ANSWERING MACHINE
         It's Hazel. Leave a message or
         don't. Your dime.

                                                        (CONTINUED)

CONTINUED:

>   CADEN
>   My love. I know how to do the
>   play. It'll take place over the
>   course of one day. The day will be
>   the day before you died, the
>   happiest day of my life. I'll be
>   able to relive it forever.

EXT. CITY STREET (INT. WAREHOUSE SET) - 2048 - NIGHT

Caden weeps inconsolably at the director's table, Michael the pre-Hazel assistant is back, neat and efficient-looking, but old now. Hazel's dog, Squishy, sleeps on the floor. The scene in the play is dull. People walk back and forth aimlessly. Various passersby on the street have hacking coughs. Tammy steps out of the bathroom, meanders over to the director's table. Hazel's sweater is on Michael's chair-back. She casually pulls it off and tries it on. Caden watches. She looks so much like Hazel now, it's unbearable. He looks away. Millicent walks by carrying a mop and bucket.

>   CADEN
>   I need a Caden for my Hazel.

>   MILLICENT
>   I... I'd very much like to play
>   Caden.

>   CADEN
>   Um...

Tammy watches intently. Millicent smiles at her.

>   MILLICENT
>   I know it would be non-traditional
>   casting, but I think I'm right for
>   it. I think I understand Caden.

>   CADEN
>   I don't understand him.

>   MILLICENT
>   Caden Cotard is a man already dead,
>   living in a half-world between
>   stasis and antistasis. Time is
>   concentrated and chronology
>   confused for him. Up until
>   recently he has strived valiantly
>   to make sense of his situation, but
>   now he has turned to stone.

(CONTINUED)

177   CONTINUED: 177

                    CADEN
          Okay. That sounds good.

                    MICHAEL
          She's right? I didn't see that at
          all. I saw it all as more hopeful.

178   INT. NYC WIG STORE - 2050 - DAY   178

       Caden and Michael look at a wig called "The Director."

                    MICHAEL
          Any thoughts for today's rehearsal?

                    CADEN
              (beat)
          I have a new title, maybe.
          <u>Infectious Diseases In Cattle</u>.

                    MICHAEL
          Huh.

                    CADEN
          The title is about a lot of things.
          You'll see. It's about a lot.
              (pause)
          Are you gay, Michael?

                    MICHAEL
          Yes. I don't see what that has to
          do with anything.

                    CADEN
          Do you know someone named Eric?

                    MICHAEL
              (defensively)
          No.

179   INT. WAREHOUSE - CEMETERY SET - 2050 - DAY   179 *

       Caden, in "Director Wig," and Michael watch Millicent,
       dressed Caden-esque, sitting at the director's table. Tammy,
       in Hazel's sweater, sits next to her. They watch the "Sammy
       Funeral" scene replayed with actors playing Tammy playing
       Hazel and an actor playing the stand-in for Sammy playing
       Caden. Tammy has her head in her hands. She looks over at
       Millicent, imploringly.

                    TAMMY
          Come over tonight? Please?

                                                        (CONTINUED)

MILLICENT
I'd like that.

CADEN
Ok, take off the sweater.

Tammy takes off the sweater, puts it on the chair back.

TAMMY
I'm hot.

MILLICENT
Yes, you are.

CADEN
Smile shyly at each other.

They do. It lingers. Millicent looks over at the funeral scene. It's dull and static.

MILLICENT
This is tedious. This is nothing.

Millicent touches Tammy's hand, heads over to the funeral scene. She whispers things to some actors, has longer conversations with others.

MICHAEL
What's she doing?

TAMMY
He's directing.

MICHAEL
She's not getting the feel of you, Caden. You don't move around. You don't talk to people. It's not --

MILLICENT
Okay, folks, let's run it!

The scene comes alive with specific activity: weeping Hazel, a little boy in the back playing with dirt clods, a man and a woman eyeing each other flirtatiously from a distance, an old woman with Parkinson's fiddling with Rosary beads, a well-dressed woman squatting and peeing near a gravesite. Soon it starts to rain. People run for cover. A young man and woman in love walk happily through the lush green field, the woman opening her mouth to the heavens. Thunder rumbles. Caden looks up, surprised that such a system is rigged here.

180 EXT. BURNING HOUSE STREET (INT. WAREHOUSE SET) - 2050 - NIGHT 180

Caden sits with Michael at the director's table and stares into space. The actors are doing what they've always done, milling, walking to and fro. Millicent, holding hands with Tammy, heads up the walk to the Hazel's house set.

                  CADEN
        Millicent.

She turns. He waves her over. Tammy sits on the stoop.

                  CADEN (CONT'D)
        That was ... spectacular.

                  MICHAEL
        It really was! Delightful!

MILLICENT	CADEN
Thanks.	I'm out of ideas. I'm dead.

                  MILLICENT
        Oh. I... could take over... as you... for a bit. Until you feel refreshed.

                  MICHAEL
        Yes! Yes!

Caden, looks sideways at Michael, remains silent.

MILLICENT	MICHAEL
I think you're tired, Caden. All these years of creative work.	Yes. I think you just need some time. To regroup.

                  CADEN
        I need to keep my hand in.

                  MILLICENT
        Well, Ellen needs to be filled.

                  CADEN
        Filled? You mean...?

MILLICENT	MICHAEL
Her role. Just for a bit.	It's a choice role. Just until you're refreshed.

(CONTINUED)

180   CONTINUED: 180

                    CADEN (CONT'D)
                (beat)
            I do like to clean.

181   INT. 31Y WALK-IN CLOSET (INT. WAREHOUSE SET) - 2050 - NIGHT   181

       Caden sits on the unmade bed and reads the note:

                    ADELE'S VOICE
            Ellen, Olive has died. It's a time
            of overwhelming grief so please
            forgive my mess; I haven't been
            able to get out of bed. Until
            today. Much affection, A.

       Caden crosses to the window and looks up at the night sky,
       even though it's clearly the ceiling of the warehouse. A
       tiny plane flies by.

182   INT. 31Y HALLWAY (INT. WAREHOUSE SET) - 2050 - NIGHT   182

       Caden walks down the hall carrying a bag of garbage to the
       incinerator chute, dumps it in, and turns back to apartment
       31Y. Old Person #2 (actor version) is standing there.

                    OLD PERSON #2 (ACTOR)
            Ellen? Is your name Ellen?

                    CADEN
            Yes?

                    OLD PERSON #2 (ACTOR)
            Caden asked me to give you this.
            You're to keep it in all the time.

       Old Person #2 (actor) hands Caden a small black button.
       Caden examines it. Old Person #2 (actor) points to his own
       ear, in which he wears one. Caden sticks it in his ear.

                    MILLICENT'S VOICE
            ... touched by the sadness of
            Adele's neighbor. So close to
            death. Reminds me of granny. I
            should really call her. Remember
            how Granny Bascomb bounced me on
            her knee pretending to be a horsie.
            I loved that so much. Say thank
            you to Adele's neighbor.

                    CADEN
            Thank you.

                                                          (CONTINUED)

182   CONTINUED: 182

                    OLD PERSON #2 (ACTOR)
                  (pause, listens, then:)
                You're very welcome, young lady.

                        MILLICENT'S VOICE
                  Now say, have a very good day.

                              CADEN
                  Have a very good day.

                    OLD PERSON #2 (ACTOR)
                  (pause, listens, then:)
                I will indeed.

183   INT. 31Y WALK-IN CLOSET (INT. WAREHOUSE SET) - 2050 - NIGHT   183

       It's dark. Caden lies in bed, attached to his pumps.

                        MILLICENT'S VOICE
                  ... miss him. Why did he have to
                  get bored with me? Everyone gets
                  bored with me. I'm not very
                  bright. And since I put on that
                  weight, I don't get the looks I
                  used to. It's not that bad. Lots
                  of people have it worse. I've got
                  a job and place to stay. Adele is
                  nice to me. And so smart and
                  talented. I don't understand her
                  artwork, but that's just me. I
                  wish I'd gone to college. I feel
                  stupid around educated people like
                  Adele. Eric was too smart for me,
                  too. We didn't talk at all near
                  the end. I'd try to tell him about
                  my day and he'd get this far away
                  look in his eyes. I kind of felt
                  sorry for him; he seemed so
                  miserable with me. I guess --

       Caden drifts off to sleep.

184   INT. ELLEN'S KITCHEN - (2050) - MORNING   184

       A tenement apartment. Ellen, in a terrycloth robe, is at the
       stove making scrambled eggs. Toast pops from the toaster and
       Ellen crosses to get it. She passes a mirror, glances at
       herself, seems momentarily surprised, pushes a wisp of hair
       behind her ear and continues to the toaster. Eric enters.
       He's an unhealthily thin middle-aged man. He doesn't
       acknowledge her, nor she him. He pours himself coffee.

                                                            (CONTINUED)

184   CONTINUED: 184

                    ELLEN
          I'm making eggs.
              (beat)
          Is everything okay, Eric?

                    ERIC
          Everything's everything.

185   INT. ELLEN'S BEDROOM - (2050) - MORNING   185

      Ellen sits on the bed with a cup of coffee and stares out the
      window. There's a city park across the street and she
      watches kids play basketball. She begins to weep.

186   EXT. FIELD - (2050) - DAY   186

      It's spring and a ten year old girl watches her mother as she
      lays out a picnic on a blanket on the ground.

                    MOTHER
          Ellen, why do you look so serious?

                    ELLEN
          I'm going to remember this moment
          for the rest of my life, mama. And
          in exactly twenty years, come here
          with my daughter and have exactly
          the same picnic.

                    MOTHER
          Baby, that's the loveliest thing
          I've ever heard.

187   INT. ELLEN'S BEDROOM - (2050) - NIGHT   187

      Ellen lies in bed watching Eric sleep next to her.

                    ELLEN
          There was supposed to be something
          else. I was to have something. A
          calm. A love. Children. A child,
          at least. Children. Meaning. I
          am always on the verge, never more
          than a tiny shove from tears. I
          can feel them in my chest now.
          That squeezing pressure. And it
          is so tempting to let go, but I am
          afraid, the next time maybe, I will
          never stop crying. I miss my
          husband even though he is lying
          here. He hates me. Oh God.
                    (MORE)

                                                              (CONTINUED)

187   CONTINUED: 187

                        ELLEN (CONT'D)
              I have disappointed him and he
              hates me. The one person who
              should be able to see me and he
              won't look. He will never look
              again.

188   INT. 31Y WALK-IN CLOSET (INT. WAREHOUSE SET) - 2050 -   188
        MORNING

        Caden lies on his back, and opens his eyes. His pumps drone.

                        CADEN
                    (quietly, mournfully)
              Eric.

        Caden looks over. No note from Adele. He gets out of bed,
        glances in the mirror, seems surprised by his reflection.

189   INT. 31Y BATHROOM (INT. WAREHOUSE SET) - 2050 - MORNING   189

        Caden sits on the toilet and pees. He wipes himself.

190   INT. APARTMENT 31Y (INT. WAREHOUSE SET) - 2051 - MORNING   190

        Caden vacuums the hall.

                        MILLICENT'S VOICE
              My period is late this month. I
              wonder what's going on. I'm
              bloated. I wish it would come.

191   OMITTED   191*

A192   INT. 31Y WALK-IN CLOSET (INT. WAREHOUSE SET) - 2051 - NIGHT A192*

        Caden stands on the ledge and uses a long brush to clean a   *
        statue's face.   *

                        MILLICENT'S VOICE   *
              Maybe I can ask Adele for a raise.   *
              It's been three years. I do a good   *
              job. God, I'm so tired tonight.   *
              I'm getting old. I'm lonely here.   *

192   EXT. POND - (2051) - DAY   192*

        An overcast sky. It's misty. The pond is very still.
        Ellen, in a heavy black coat, sits in an old row boat.
        Something pokes out of the water near her, then disappears.
        She leans over the edge to see and falls in.

A193   INT. POND (UNDERWATER) - (2051) - SAME   A193

She sinks to the bottom It's murky. She walks along the muddy bottom with no difficulty breathing. There's a small house; its windows aglow with firelight.

B193   INT. POND CABIN - (2051) - CONTINUOUS   B193

Ellen enters. There's a man with blond hair. It's not underwater anymore.

                    ELLEN
          Hi. I was walking by and --

                    BLOND MAN
          It's okay.

He approaches and strokes her hair, gently puts an arm around her waist. She sighs and moves in to him. He kisses her. She touches his chest, which is now shirtless. Now they're on the floor of the cabin. It's stone and Ellen's naked buttocks are pushed against it as the man has sex with her. She wraps a legs around him. The man's face is close.

                    BLOND MAN (CONT'D)
          Ellen.

193   INT. 31Y WALK-IN CLOSET (INT. WAREHOUSE SET) - 2051 -   193
       MORNING

Caden awakens. He switches off his pumps.

                    MILLICENT'S VOICE
          I remember the dream. I try to
          hold onto it. So lovely. If only
          my life. Who was he? Nobody I
          know. Yet I know him so well. Is
          he anywhere in this world? The man
          who says my name.

A tear forms in Caden's eye, falls down the side of his face.

                    MILLICENT'S VOICE (CONT'D)
          Get up. Look at the night table
          for a note from Adele.

Caden gets up and glances at the night table. A type-written note:

(CONTINUED)

193   CONTINUED: 193

                              MALE VOICE
                    Adele died of lung cancer last
                    night. You may stay on if you
                    like.

                              MILLICENT'S VOICE
                    Look shocked. Weep.

         Caden looks shocked, then weeps.

                              MILLICENT'S VOICE (CONT'D)
                    Go into the kitchen and --

         The voice stops. Caden stops. He waits. Nothing. He takes
         out the earpiece and looks at it, shakes it, then slips it
         back in his ear. Nothing. He waits. In the distance he
         hears wailing and gun shots.

194   INT. 31Y WALK-IN CLOSET (INT. WAREHOUSE SET) - 2053 - NIGHT 194

         The lights are out. Caden sits on the bed, still waiting.

195   INT. 31Y WALK-IN CLOSET (INT. WAREHOUSE SET) - 2055 - DAY   195

         Caden sits on the bed, his head slumped against the
         headboard, sleeping. Distant explosions wake him. He opens
         his eyes and sits up straight, and waits. He taps his ear.

196   INT. 31Y HALLWAY (INT. WAREHOUSE SET) - 2055 - NIGHT   196

         The hall is very dark. Caden exits apartment 31Y. Old
         person #2 (actor) stands in the hallway and faces away,
         unmoving. Caden walks past and nods. Old person #2 does not
         respond. Caden presses the elevator button.

                              OLD PERSON #2 (ACTOR)
                    There's nobody running it anymore.

         Caden looks at Old Person #2 and nods.

197   INT. WAREHOUSE - 31Y BUILDING STAIRWELL - 2055 - CONTINUOUS 197

         Dark. The unfinished, back-of-a-facade of the set is
         apparent. Caden walks down endless plywood stairs. The
         bowels of the building: fake water pipes, electrical cords.

198   EXT. CITY STREET (INT. WAREHOUSE SET) - 2055 - MORNING   198

         No lights. Vague daylight drifts in from high warehouse
         windows, from which cardboard has fallen. Deadly quiet,
         abandoned. Caden passes the occasional body on the street.
         Fires smolder in buildings.

                                                              (CONTINUED)

198   CONTINUED: 198

      The streets are flooded with sewer water. Buildings are draped with massive tarps. Behind a fence are piles of bodies.

A199   EXT. BURNING HOUSE (INT. WAREHOUSE SET) - 2055 - MORNING   A199

      He passes the Hazel's House set, burnt to the ground.

B199   EXT. WAREHOUSE STREET (INT. WAREHOUSE SET) - 2055 - MORNING B199

      He arrives at the warehouse set and enters.

199   EXT. CITY STREET (INT. WAREHOUSE-WITHIN-WAREHOUSE SET) -   199
      2055 - MORNING

      Deserted here too. The same occasional fires, flooding, dead bodies.

A200   EXT. WAREHOUSE STREET (INT. WAREHOUSE-WITHIN-WAREHOUSE SET) A200
      - 2055 - MORNING

      Caden walks, soon arriving at the warehouse set within the warehouse set. He enters.

200   EXT. CITY STREET (INT. WAREHOUSE-WITHIN-WAREHOUSE-WITHIN-   200
      WAREHOUSE SET) - 2055 - MORNING

      Another dark, deserted street, more bodies, fires, floods. Caden panics. He pulls out his earpiece, shakes it, and puts it back. He walks.

A201   EXT. WAREHOUSE STREET (INT. WAREHOUSE-WITHIN-WAREHOUSE-   A201
      WITHIN-WAREHOUSE SET) - 2055

      He arrives at the warehouse within the warehouse within the warehouse. He enters.

201   EXT. CITY STREET (INT. WAREHOUSE-WITHIN-WAREHOUSE-WITHIN-   201
      WAREHOUSE-WITHIN-WAREHOUSE SET) - 2055 - DAY

      Deserted. Caden walks. He gets in a golf cart and drives through the deserted street sets.

202   EXT. BEACH (INT. WAREHOUSE-WITHIN-WAREHOUSE-WITHIN-   202
      WAREHOUSE-WITHIN-WAREHOUSE SET) - 2055 - CONTINUOUS

      Caden reaches the beach set, and drives the cart on the sand. He sees footprints. He gets out and follows them, spots a woman ahead walking with a suitcase. He hurries as much as he can with his limp, his weakness, his ancient body, to catch up with her.

(CONTINUED)

CADEN
Hello.

The woman turns. She's middle-aged, face radiating kindness.

CADEN (CONT'D)
Where is everybody?

WOMAN
Mostly dead. Some have left.

CADEN
Would you sit with me for a moment? I'm very tired. And lonely.

The woman smiles at Caden. They sit on a log.

CADEN (CONT'D)
I feel like I know you.

WOMAN
I was the mother in Ellen's dream. Perhaps from there.

CADEN
Yes! That's it. Yes. You seem a bit older than I remember.

WOMAN
(chuckling)
That dream was quite a while ago.

He's silent. The woman touches his hand.

CADEN
I didn't mean to say you look old.

WOMAN
I know.

CADEN
Everyone's dreams in all those apartments. All those secrets we'll never know. That's the truth of it -- all the thoughts nobody will ever know.

WOMAN
It's true.

(CONTINUED)

                    CADEN
          I'm sorry the experiment didn't
          work. I wanted it to with all my
          heart. I wanted to do that picnic
          with my daughter. I feel I've
          disappointed you terribly.

                    WOMAN
          No. No. I am so proud of you.

Caden starts to tear up.

                    CADEN
          All I want is someone to see me,
          someone to look at me with
          kindness. For me to be the most
          special person in the world to just
          one person.

                    WOMAN
          I know, baby. I know.

He looks at her tentatively. She's looking into his eyes
directly, clearly, kindly. She smiles.

                    WOMAN (CONT'D)
          You're going to be fine.

Caden starts to weep so hard he chokes. Strings of snot pour
from his nose. The woman holds him, gently takes off his
wig, and strokes his sparse hair. He looks out over her
shoulder at the dark empty city at the far end of the
warehouse. His rheumy eyes light up.

                    CADEN
          I know what to do with this play
          now. I have an idea. I think --

The screen goes black fast.

                         END

Q & A

WITH CHARLIE KAUFMAN
BY ROB FELD

When I first heard you were making Synecdoche, New York—*which was untitled at the time—it was just spoken of as a horror movie, with Spike Jonze directing. You eventually decided to direct it yourself, and, while the film is terrifying existentially, of course, it's not a genre horror film. Was that your original intent and did it evolve into something else?*

Charlie Kaufman: No, I think my original intention was to never do a genre movie. It was more to try and think of what is scary to me. I don't know if that's ultimately what I made, but certainly more than a genre film, it was to think about things that are troubling in the real world and work with that. At the time Spike and I pitched it, Amy Pascal at Sony had said she wanted to do a horror movie with us, and she basically didn't care what it was. She wanted to give us freedom. The way I've always worked, especially in the last few scripts, has been to start and let the thing evolve. I don't have it outlined, so I don't know where it's going or how it's going to end. So, to say that it was at that time what it became would be impossible, but I don't think it's gone far afield in terms of things I was interested in, either illness, fear of death, loneliness, lack of meaning in life, guilt, passage of time. I think those are all things that I came into it with.

Rob Feld interviewed Charlie Kaufman in Pasadena, California, on July 22, 2008. Feld is a screenwriter whose writings on film and interviews with noted filmmakers appear regularly in such publications as the Writers and Directors Guild journals, *Written By* and *DGA Quarterly*, as well as in the Newmarket Press Shooting Script® series.

And how did the story itself start to develop? Did you have notions of terrifying things and then start piecing them together to become a whole?

CK: It's so tricky to use the term *terrifying* because I think, early on, it stopped being part of what I was thinking about. I found that when I started to think of things that would be perceived as terrifying, it felt very manipulative. It's kind of like when a cat jumps out in a horror movie, you know what I mean? At that point, it just becomes, What do you do to make that scary? And then it doesn't have anything to do with anything. It immediately falls into that sort of genre crap, and I wasn't interested in that. So it started out with illness, death, and relationship problems—which may be in everything that I do—and then I let it develop. It took a few years to write it.

Were you talking to Spike about things at the time? Was he contributing?

CK: No, the basic idea of Adele leaving and Caden never seeing her or his daughter again was built into the beginning. There was the issue of illness; getting sicker and sicker and trying to find some way of proving himself, his value; of feeling a lack of confidence and self-doubt in his work brought about by Adele, her leaving, and her lack of interest in his work. He was trying to somehow prove something in a vacuum, in a way, because she's not even there anymore. But in terms of the specifics, I don't really remember any more than that.

You worked with a string of very smart actors on this film. What was your collaborative process with them?

CK: They're all great actors I like, and really like working with them all, but working with each of them is different. They're different people, and every relationship with anybody is different. Some people wanted to talk a lot and some didn't, but they certainly all contributed enormously to the process with what they brought. I think that's always true. I've always felt that the actors make it alive.

Did things change and evolve as you started talking to them and they started finding their characters?

CK: A little bit, not a lot. There are lines that changed, there are lines that people improvised. But there's Caden and Hazel on paper and then there's Caden and Hazel being played by Phillip Hoffman and Samantha Morton, and that's a different thing. What *that* feels like suddenly becomes a major issue. You have one issue when you're writing dialogue, and you have this other issue when you have personalities and chemistry between people. So you take what it is that you started with and then you see what works; there are things that get cut out or don't play the way you want them to or you thought they would, or maybe there's a developing dynamic between two people that can be played up. And then there's how you edit the movie when it's done.

I think it's definitely a big learning process when you're making a movie. You get more and more experience with these characters as the days go by. For example, I wanted to shoot as much as possible in chronological order for a bunch of reasons, not the least of which was that Phil's character ages forty years and you don't want to throw him into being a ninety-year-old man the first day. He didn't want to do that, and I certainly didn't want to do it. But in addition to that, we were able to schedule it in such a way that we were able to shoot all of Phil's relationship with Catherine Keener up front, the first thing we did. That served a bunch of purposes. One is that there's an almost mundane tone to those scenes compared to the rest of the movie, which was a good place to start. It's a relationship. Phil and Catherine know each other because they did *Capote* together. They're friends and comfortable with each other, and they did a lot of improvisation—not on-screen so much, but in rehearsal—to establish the relationship between these two characters. You come into the relationship at the end of it, but there's the implication that there's a long history, that they know each other very well, and I wanted to feel that on-screen.

I felt like it worked very well, not only in establishing their relationship but giving Caden the basis for everything that was coming after. I think his feeling of being unmoored worked partially because we started with them together. We came in and did all this work but then, all of a sudden, Catherine was gone. The experience of making this movie was so intense, the days were so long and Phil worked so hard, that Phil and I would say to each other two weeks after Catherine was done shooting, "God, it feels like seven years since we saw Catherine." We both felt it and there was a real sadness to it, which I really, really think helped. And that wasn't planned. That was just lucky. I think it was a combination of the comfortableness of the early scenes and then how hard this shoot was. It made it feel that every day was five days ago. So that worked really well.

There is this one scene that stayed with me, or at least jumped out at me, both times I saw the film: the one where Phil comes back after his play opens to find Catherine and Jennifer there, stoned. It's a simple scene but it's very layered. There's so much going on.

CK: Yeah, I love that scene. They're great. It just came together so well—I think that's the first scene that came together when we were cutting the movie. We just didn't have to touch it, it was so good.

Was there much to talk about with them on that one? Was there some improv? How did it come together day-of?

CK: Well, it was very early, obviously, because it was while Catherine was still there. It was the first thing we did with Jennifer. You know, I just think it was on the page, they knew what they were playing, and the actors are really good. I think that's what it is. Then it's a straightforward scene to play. I loved the scene when I wrote it, and I feel like it played the way I pictured it. Catherine is really great; she's second-guessing herself in everything, her anger and her dismissal, which I think is a real thing. She's kind of behaving awfully in that scene, but she's not in any way a demon or a villain.

As a director, how did you communicate big-picture ideas like tone with your cast, director of photography, and editor?

CK: With Phil, who I spent the most time with before and during the shoot—he was in virtually every scene in the movie, with two minor exceptions, when Hazel was by herself—we talked a lot but really about the character, aging, illness, and relationships, on a very personal level. I think we got to know each other that way. I talked to the production designer and the DP about the things I wanted to feel and the point of view of the movie. I very much wanted to emphasize that it was from Caden's point of view. It's a very personal experience, so there's really little in the way it's shot that isn't from Caden's point of view. There's one moment in the movie toward the end where you have a bird's-eye view of him walking down the street when he's very old, but that's it. Everything else is seen as he sees it, which is a very specific choice, maybe even more than I realized.

We couldn't, and do not, have any establishing shots in this movie, not one, with the exception of that bird's-eye view, if you could call it that. And so it gives it a sort of uncomfortable feeling, I think—and maybe not for the good of the movie, I don't know—but it was decided that we wouldn't have them. And then we had to make decisions based on the enormous constraints of time and money. So we had to shoot it in a certain way, build only certain things, figure out how to fake the rest of it with special effects, and even then how to get the most out of the effects that we could afford. We shot 204 scenes in 45 days, which is, I think, physically impossible.

With a higher budget, how would you have shot it differently?

CK: I would have had twenty-five or forty-five more days to give me time with the actors because of all the different scenes and setups we had. We had to move more quickly than I would have liked. I think we did pretty well, but if we had more money to build sets, we could have exposed this world in a bigger way. Again, I wanted to make it very personal and to make it Caden's story, but I had all sorts of coverage issues because that takes time. We had to be very economical in shooting, and I think with more time I would have had more to choose from in the editing room. I would have had more time to think about what I wanted things to look like, whereas I had to be somewhat conservative because you've got to get what you've got to get and then you have to move on. So that became a modus operandi of the production. I am happy with the way the movie looks, and I think I learned a lot. This was an amazing education for me. If I ever do this again, I think I'll have the opportunity to experiment in different ways.

I've been wondering about the development of the title, Synecdoche, New York. It's kind of perfect and so clever, but you had to have known what you were writing before you found it.

CK: I had a bunch of titles as I was working on it and this was one. I don't know—I liked it the most. It isn't the cleverness that ultimately sold me on it; it felt mysterious and slightly creepy to me, I don't even know why. That appealed to me, but I don't think it feels that way to other people.

I don't get "creepy" from it, but I'm stuck on the chicken-and-egg thing. Again, you had to have known what you were writing before the title occurred to you.

CK: Not necessarily.

But then it wouldn't mean anything.

CK: Well, I don't know at what stage it came…You know what's so funny? God, I hate the Internet. Here's what happened: we were so careful about not letting the screenplay get out and seen by people, or stolen and put online.

But somehow that happened, and in so doing the title page got taken off. This is my sort of detective work in guessing what happened here, but I imagine somebody retyped the title page as *Schenectady, New York*. So, now, in the lovely world of the Internet, people say—and it just becomes part of the truth of the story—that the original title of this movie was *Schenectady, New York*, and that somehow along the way I decided to change it to *Synecdoche*. The title was never *Schenectady, New York*. It is not a title I would ever use for anything. I mean, what the hell would I use that for? So, in the lore of the Internet, I changed it after I realized that there was a play on words here, but no, I didn't. But sometimes things are serendipitous. You're working on something and then you find out that it kind of connects in ways you didn't anticipate. I don't know; I don't remember, honestly. When I was going to turn in the script, I went over my list with some people, asking what they liked, and people seemed to gravitate toward this.

Caden has endless problems finding a title for his own work, so I'm wondering about the problem of meaning in general, of relying on a signifier like a word to convey meaning where language fails. Is everything just a poor approximation?

CK: Sure. Funny, I had this conversation with Amy Pascal when we were talking about this movie early on, and I was still writing it for Sony. I was explaining something that I had been going through, some kind of depression or really, really anxious experience that related to the story in the movie. And I said that what was interesting to me was that, when I was going through it, I couldn't talk about it. The very act of talking about it has made it obvious that I'm not going through it anymore. There is this preverbal or nonverbal kind of thing that is the really-felt thing, and once you start to translate it into words, it loses its immediacy or its power. And so, yeah, I think that that's true. It's definitely an approximation, and I struggle with that a lot when I'm writing because my things tend to be very wordy. I *like* words.

Is there a point where the aesthetic representation of our experience just kind of fails? Does it always fall short?

CK: Yeah, but I think it's inherent to the species and I don't think we can do anything else. Metaphor is how we communicate. There's no other way to do it. When you're trying to explain something to somebody else, you have to say, "It's like this." If they haven't experienced it and you want them to understand it, you have to equate it to something that they do understand, and that's what language allows you to do. You can't do it any other way. You could do it with visual art, I guess. I think there's a real value to metaphor or analogy, but it isn't the *thing*.

After Eternal Sunshine *but before finishing* Synecdoche, *you wrote and staged two one-act radio plays,* Theater for the New Ear, *to Carter Burwell's music. They were staged readings, but you directed them yourself. What did you take from that experience or how did it inform* Synecdoche?

CK: I took Phil from that experience—who did a companion one-act written by the Coen Brothers—but on a very pragmatic level, I took from it a little bit of confidence. I mean, the idea that I could actually go into a situation and direct Meryl Streep is not something that would have been conceivable to me a few years ago. I wouldn't have even been able to talk to her. But she listened to me, took my direction, and seemed to not hate me. And the thing came out well, I thought. I really liked working with the actors and I think they liked working with me, so I felt like I had that going into this.

Did the fact that it was first staged at St. Ann's Warehouse in Brooklyn have anything to do with the fact that Caden's play is put up in a Brooklyn warehouse?

CK: No, that was already written. I was in the midst of writing this thing and kind of stuck when Carter approached me. I kind of thought it might free me up a little bit to do something else, and I would feel somehow that the three years in between wouldn't have been totally wasted. Ever since I was young, I've had the idea of creating a massive replica of something, and it being minutely detailed in the reproduction of it. I always have liked sets. When I went to plays in New York when I was a kid, there might be a set of a tenement apartment, and they might put dirty fingerprints around where the light switch is, for example. I *love* that stuff, I don't know why. I'd just be, like, *Wow, they've got fingerprints there!* Or, *That's so cool the way they make the set paint look like it's peeling.* In *Synecdoche*, we shot Claire's New York apartment in a real apartment in Dumbo, so we had the real version of the apartment but also the mock-up version built on the third floor of the scaffolding of Caden's set. You would go up there and it was an *exact* replica. If you didn't look this way where there's nothing but a big drop, you wouldn't know that you weren't in the real place. It's this old New York apartment and the floors were exactly the same, and it was gorgeous.

I don't know why, but that stuff is so exciting to me. And I think that was as big an influence on my wanting to write this as anything. I remember when I was in college I used to ride home on the F train, where it went above ground in Brooklyn, and look out and imagine that it was this thing that I had built and that all these people were actors and such. I think that if I'd had a bigger budget, I could have made people feel more of that giant version of the set, with thousands and thousands of people in it.

What can you do in theater that you can't in film, and what's Caden trying to do? What's your experience of theater, in that sense?
CK: The thing you can do in theater that you can't do in film is change it. And interact with the audience. That's what it has going for it, which is why I try to do that in film when I can, in sort of another way, having stuff be layered so that you can watch it again and feel like it's a different experience. But I think that's the main thing. It's always different and it's very hard to realize that because we're so used to watching movies and television, but you can watch a play and forget that this is actually happening as you're watching it. There is a certain kind of terror in that reality, for the actors and for me as an audience member.

It's so funny, I was doing the *New Ear* play and with a group of people talking about actors going up on their lines in theater. And Meryl said something like, "That's the most exciting thing." It never really occurred to me that an actor would feel that way. I used to act in plays and the idea of forgetting my lines, which has happened to me, is so terrifying, and I love the idea of approaching it from the other way; that this is actually kind of a cool thing to happen and watch because you're watching this thing, someone maneuver within it, and the other people on stage maneuver and figure out what they need to do, and suddenly you're awake.

I guess that's the difference, and I'm sure there are others. What was cool about the *New Ear* piece to me is that the play stops in real time and the actor yells at the audience, and in a movie you can't do that because they're not really yelling at you; they're yelling at an imagined audience or an audience that's on film with them. You don't feel the threat that you feel when you're at a magic show and you're terrified that the guy's going to pick on you.

As surreal as Synecdoche is, you don't have the characters behaving in nonsensical ways, it seems to me. I mean, I feel like they come from emotionally

real places. You referenced Pinter, Beckett (with Krapp's Last Tape*), and Kafka (with* The Trial*), and you're working in an Existentialist voice, but where an ancillary character in a Kafka piece might come up with something out of left field, your characters are largely emotionally consistent.*

CK: I hope that what you're saying is true. In everything I write I try to have the characters grounded in how this person would react in this situation, otherwise there's no point doing it. Otherwise there's no reason for it to exist, in my mind. It just becomes unrelatable. In Kafka I see the characters doing the same thing. The situation is absurd, but they have something that they need and they're trying to get it.

The protagonist, yes, but the peripheral characters might come in and throw a curveball.

CK: Right, right, right.

And I don't feel yours doing that in that sort of way. You have that one line when Caden asks the doctor if it's serious, and he replies, "We don't know, but yes."

CK: Yeah, but it isn't also, because to me that's the way doctors are. I mean, I think it's funny, hopefully, but that's the relationship I often feel with doctors; you're scared and they've got this God-like arrogance, and you feel like you're this wormy little sick thing. My favorite thing is when I find a doctor who tells me something is physically wrong with him. It's so rare, but it's happened on occasion and it's like, *wow*, because I'm surprised. Of course he's a human being and he's going to have whatever physical problems he has—he's not a god—but I can't get it through my head that they're not, and I think they love that, I think they foster it.

But, yeah, for any character I write, I need to feel like I'm writing from their point of view, so even if what they do is absurd, when I write it I have to know why they're doing it. Otherwise it becomes sort of silly to me. If you don't do that, it's a little Lewis Carroll or something, which there's nothing wrong with, obviously, but...

Actually Hope Davis's character does some of that, too, but she's a doctor as well.

CK: She's a doctor, yes. But I feel like she's... I think she's a really *bad* therapist. *[Laughter]* Yeah, she does it, I guess.

I guess I felt that if there was one rule in the Synecdoche ***universe you created, it was like anything can happen, utter absurdity can happen, but that emotional link to reality will be maintained or relatable.***

CK: Yeah, if you look at the movie like a dream—which is kind of how I thought of it—things can happen that are not naturalistic in a dream, but they've got emotional resonance. And I don't know if I was successful in that, but that was my goal…if you don't know why Hazel lives in a burning house, you might still be able to feel something because of it.

Metaphors seem to operate subconsciously as well, even if you can't verbalize their effect on us.

CK: Well, yeah, I think that's what dreams do. I'm so astounded by dreams, by my dreams, because I feel like I do my best writing in them, and I'm doing it in real time, or what seems to me to be real time. Like what you were saying about the title, *Synecdoche*, about which came first; I often have dreams that have a surprise ending that works! And it's, like, *How the hell did I do that?* because *I'm* doing it. I'm thinking that I figure it out in real time, that all these pieces came together. I can't possibly have it planned for the dream to arrive at this surprise ending, because then I would know what it was, and then it wouldn't be a surprise. But you get somewhere and there's a reveal and it's like, *Oh, fuck!* As opposed to something that takes me three years to write when I'm awake, I can write a dream in my sleep in a matter of moments.

We're all brilliant artists in our subconscious, constructing these metaphors that we can't necessarily in our conscious lives.

CK: Yeah. I mean, I think it's really hard, or we don't know how to approach it to do it.

Do you use any of your actual dream elements in your writing?

CK: No, not that I'm aware of. But I think about structural things about dreams, and in some cases try to duplicate that, more than specific plot points or incidents—like, how things can move, or how you can be here and then be there, and how things can change, and how people can change. I think Hope's character, the way she becomes this other thing on the airplane, to me was intended to be dreamlike, sort of like an anxiety dream. But the way time passes in the story, the way Caden can't find his wife, is a very obvious dream thing. You know that feeling of not being able to get through to people on the telephone, or that kind of thing? I have that dream a lot. I have elevator dreams a lot and there seems to be elevators in almost everything that I write, I realize.

No monkeys in this one, though.
CK: I don't think I had monkeys in the last one, either.

No, you didn't.
CK: No, I'm through with monkeys.

Speaking of the way time moves, you've thought about it and our experience of that a good deal. Has your own experience of time changed?
CK: Yeah! I mean, I definitely tried to convey that in the movie. I feel like as I get older, it moves much faster. I feel like it's always about to be my birthday or Christmas or tax day. Every tax day I'm so ill prepared, and I have to scrounge around, find everything and get it ready. I vow to myself it will be different next year, and then next week it's next year, and I haven't kept things in order and I do it again. So, yeah, that element of time connects obviously to mortality and feelings of impending doom.

How does time function for Caden in a family scenario, as opposed to maybe after Adele leaves? What does time look like in that experience?
CK: Well, it's moving. In the very first sequence in the movie—I don't know if you've noticed this, but the day keeps changing. The dates on the newspaper keep changing, the milk goes sour. When he has the accident with the sink, it's Christmas at the doctor's office, it's New Year's on the ride home, and when he goes to the ophthalmologist, he thanks him for getting him in so quickly, but on the calendar behind him it says March 2006. So there's all that sort of stuff going on and one of those things I think a lot of people won't catch the first time, but I like that. I like that experience of finding things in movies. So, I think that's Caden's experience, and after Adele and Olive leave, he keeps thinking Olive is the same age; he thinks his wife's been gone a week, but he learns from Hazel that it's been a year. When he goes to Berlin, he finds out from Maria that Olive is now eleven. The next time he goes to Berlin, she's a stripper. Another dreamlike thing is that, for some reason, Olive keeps writing in her diary, even though she's not there anymore.

Caden's never happy where he is, either. He doesn't really exist in his moment.

CK: No, but who does? I mean, maybe somebody does. *Is* there a moment? I don't think there is. I've heard and tried a lot to do this "present moment" thing, in meditation and stuff, but there is no present moment. That's my new conclusion.

***Synecdoche** explores many of the themes you have in the past, and also tries to find ways to depict our actual experience of things, but in a more externalized way, maybe, than your other films.*

CK: Well, sort of. I set out to do that. I set out to *not* have voice-over in this movie, for example. In order to have the internal experience of the character, which I'm interested in, I decided to project it externally, so that's why the world is interacting with him the way it is. It echoes back to it being the dream state that he's in, even though I don't see this movie as a dream. But it is using dream logic and that kind of symbolism and stuff. But, yeah, it was a conscious decision not to have voice-over—the only voice-over that exists in the movie is in the form of other people talking to him, like Millicent instructing him in somebody else's interior monologue.

It made me think about how one's reaction to the outside world is totally subject to what one is feeling at that very moment.

CK: Yeah, of course. Your brain chemistry is creating the exterior world. It doesn't exist the way you see it. Colors don't exist the way you see them. The world doesn't have colors. It's just your brain interpreting them in different ways.

And then I was relating that to the world falling apart outside the warehouse as things deteriorated inside it, or maybe it's the other way around, but one reflecting the other.

CK: Who knows? But, yeah, they're reflecting each other.

Again, you referenced Beckett, Kafka, and Pinter in the piece itself; did you set out to work in this Existentialist tradition?

CK: No, I don't set out to do anything. I guess I have a certain kind of interest and background. The reason that Pinter is in there is, when I started to write that first scene, I wanted to set it in a real world and then move into this more interior world. So, for that date when that supposedly takes place, I went to the front page of the *New York Times*. Pinter won the Nobel

Prize that day, and I had the same reaction as Caden. I looked and thought, *Oh, fuck, Pinter's died*. So I put that in. That runner who's referenced in that scene died that day, and there was avian flu found in Turkey. All that stuff is real, it was October 15 whatever year—2005, maybe. So the Pinter thing was an accident, which is funny because reviews were saying how the whole movie is obviously an homage to Pinter, and it's like, *No, it's not*. But people do that all the time. You know, they're also saying it's an homage to *8?*, and no one seems to believe me that I've never seen *8?*. Apparently there's a big set or something, and it's about the women in Fellini's life. The other thing they say is that it's referencing *All That Jazz*, which is a movie I've also never seen.

But there are conventions that you seem to at least draw on of that form, from Pinter and Beckett, like the verbal miscues.

CK: Well, it's not conscious, but I've been influenced by those guys. I've been influenced by Ionesco, Pirandello, I've read a lot of Kafka…but, I mean, other people do that sort of thing, too. I've been influenced by Woody Allen, Monty Python. You just read stuff that you relate to that makes sense to you. I think you read certain things when you're a kid and you feel like it articulates something that you've thought, or it even gives you permission to do something like that. Like when I read *Six Characters in Search of an Author*, it was like, *Oh, fuck, you can do that? That is so cool! That's eye-opening*.

How does humor function in Synecdoche, **or how did you approach its use? There's a great deal of it, but you don't punch it.**

CK: No, I don't. I think it goes back to the idea that I want everything to feel like it's justified within the story or the emotions of the characters. So I don't think there are any jokes in this script that are just jokes, but I feel like *Eternal Sunshine* is the same way. I was trying not to have anything just there as a punch line. I think *Being John Malkovich* and *Human Nature* are different in that there are jokes in those movies. Which is fun to write, but I still don't think that they're like sitcoms.

There are many elements to the film that function as metaphors in one way or another—for example, the burning house. How much are you thinking of such things as metaphors, and precisely what you want to evoke with them, and how much is it subconscious—you get an image, it feels right, and you go with it?

CK: I think that it's the latter. I'll have a feeling about a quality that comes from this image. It affects me in a certain way, in a general way. The name of my production company is Projective Testing Service. Projective tests are psychological tests, of which Rorschach is an example, but the ones I'm more interested in present a series of ambiguous scenes that you're asked to describe. I feel like if I get too specific with the metaphors, it limits somebody else's opportunity to take it and make it theirs. A lot of people come up to me and say that they don't have any idea why the burning house is there. But one guy in particular, who worked on the movie, was so moved by this house. He feels like it's such a reflection of his experience in life, it means something really profound to him. And I like that, I want that. I want that to be available to people.

So if I'm moved by something or affected by something or feel charged by an idea, to take it and make it too much mine is not necessarily anything I want to do. I feel like it works in this movie because it's a dreamlike reality to me, but when something like that presents itself in a dream, you can adjust to it as the dreamer very easily. If something unrealistic happens in a dream, what tends to happen is that I will explain it to myself within the dream: *Oh, well, yeah, that can happen because of this.* Then you just go on with it. I wanted to have that kind of thing. It's not like you're fixated on how she can live in a burning house for the whole movie. It's like, *She lives in a burning house, let's move on*, and it will continue to burn and that's where she lives. And, consequently, this guy was really affected by it and that, to me, is great.

As I was reading the script I was struck by the sense of carnality and human viscera, and, out of curiosity, I started jotting down words: blood, feces, piss, poop, urine, dump, veins, capillaries, "boy parts," bumps, plumbing, pipes, teeth, raw nerve, swollen calves, vomit, seizure, saliva, gum surgery…

CK: Well, it's real stuff and we don't ever have it in movies, so I decided to put it in just for fun. Yeah, we actually had more feces in the movie that has made it to the screen. Did you put down vaginal juices?

I did, yeah: nocturnal emissions, saliva, digestive, penis, vagina, lips, eyes, genital mutilation, rape, tattoos, scar, murder, defecate, snot, masturbation, violent sex, menstrual blood….*I think maybe with the exception of spinal fluid, you got everything. There's no bile, but I was willing to include that in vomit.*

CK: It wasn't calculated. The feces was calculated. I actually said to myself that every movie I do seems to have a masturbation scene in it, so this movie will not have any masturbation. I feel like I've kind of conquered that taboo, but now I'm going to do the feces.

I want to go back to the idea of art, in general, and Caden's attempts toward it. What do you think is success in art, and does it always fall short?

CK: Well, I don't know. Woody Allen said it always falls short, which I remember reading when I was younger and thinking that I liked that he said that. You never quite get what you want. And that's why you keep working. I'm sure that's true, but I can think of some great works of art that come pretty damn close, so…but I don't know what the artist's intentions were.

Martha Graham had this great phrase, "sublime dissatisfaction."

CK: Yeah, you know, speaking of dancers, Isadora Duncan has a line that I really like, "I've strived my entire life to make one authentic gesture," which I think is a great notion. I think it's a really hard thing to do, maybe impossible.

Does Caden finally do that by dying?

CK: I haven't thought of it that way. I don't know. That being a criterion, I think we have plenty of authentic gestures. I think what we do to communicate and express our experience to others is where we fall short. But I do think there are amazing things out there; it's very hard to see them now, I think, because everything is so commodified. It's very hard to know what you're looking at and what the significance of anything is; how much real stuff is being done that you will never see because it hasn't been co-opted and sold?

Caden's MacArthur gives him the freedom to do any project he wants. Did you feel that sense at that time? You had great success with **Eternal Sunshine,** *and you were given seeming carte blanche by Sony to go do something.*

CK: No, within that dreamlike world I wanted to give him the freedom, and I thought getting a MacArthur was funny…and I was trying to goad the committee into giving me one because I've mentioned them. I actually think I blew any chance I might have by doing this, especially finding the most absurdly German-sounding person to read the letter.

The minister's soliloquy...
CK: Yeah, it's not in the script.

It's not in the script, and it's an amazing statement of pain. Tell me where that came from.
CK: I wrote it the day before. I had some notes about it in my computer, and I really didn't know what I wanted to do with that scene. I wanted Millicent to replace Caden as director and do something that was stylistically completely different than he would ever do. I wanted it to be mind-blowing for Caden, to feel like he would never write anything like that. The speech is completely on the nose and presentational. I was trying to do something in the form of choreography instead, but when it came to the day, I didn't have anything. I had a bunch of extras, didn't know what I was going to do, so I put this thing together and hired this actor, Chris Evan Welch, who had auditioned for the movie and I really liked, but I hadn't had anything for. I was looking for someone who had the stage chops to do this, and at the time he was playing Mercutio in *Romeo and Juliet* in Central Park. He got the two pages of monologue the night before, came in, and was just great. He had the whole thing memorized perfectly and delivered it in such a dynamic way, it was like, *Oh my God, this is actually going to work*, even though it was completely counterintuitive to have that kind of speech late in the movie by a character you've never seen before and will never see again. It was intended to be effective but not *good*.

Because it's too on the nose?
CK: Often I might give myself permission to write something I wouldn't normally if it's housed in a certain context and not supposed to be coming from *me*. I did it in *Adaptation* with the speech that Donald gives to Charlie at the log: *You are what you love.* And I actually believe that Donald thing, but I would never say it sincerely because I'd be embarrassed.

But it is what the whole movie was about, in a sense.
CK: Yeah, but it also is so on the nose and so Hallmark. And you can be affected by things like that, and Charlie is affected by it, which is true. I can be affected by really corny movies all the time and often I am. So that's where the preacher speech came from, but the impetus for it was to have Caden—who's completely exhausted and has tried to maintain integrity in the way that he would direct this massive project—be so affected and

floored by something that is so on the nose with its moral and lesson, and delivered as a speech.

Let's talk about the ending. My obvious associations while watching Caden obey disembodied, staticky, and sporadic instructions from Millicent in his ear were to an absent or nonsensical god and to an idea of submission for him at that point.

CK: Yeah. I think there's a few things going on there. I think that there's something that happens in real life when people get old. It's a non-dramatic moment for them, after their spouse dies or something, there's this period of waiting and not being the center of the world in any way anymore; being kind of pushed aside. People stop being interested in you, and you're just sort of waiting it out.

Are you no longer the lead character in your own story?

CK: You're no longer the lead character in any story, yeah. And I think there's that element to what's happening. Caden's being told what to do—he's being told what the sadnesses of his life are, but they're not even the sadnesses of *his* life. They're of somebody else's life that he's submitting to. But I think everyone's going through the same thing, with different specifics and in different timelines. You're at *this* point in your timeline, while somebody else is at *that* point in their timeline, or someone's getting to *another* point, but it's basically the same timeline. You start here and you go there. You grow up and you get old and you get sick and you die, and you have your sadnesses and your frustrations and your loneliness and all of those things. And I guess to me there is a growth in knowing that and recognizing the parallel between your experience and other people's experience, and that there really is, in a larger, philosophical sense, not only a parallel but you really *are* the other person.

I think we get very caught up in sort of protecting our identity and not looking at how we don't live in isolation from anything else in the world. It's very much like if you're an artist, the thing that you know if you're doing a painting is that there's positive and there's negative space, and positive and negative space don't exist without the other. It's not like you paint a person and they're just there. They're existing within the context of everything else in the painting, and that's true of us literally and that's true of us figuratively. *You* don't exist in any way outside of my brain. I mean, you exist in many other people's brains, but how you exist for me is my interpretation of that, and vice versa. And who knows what that means? I think it's much more complicated than we can ever know, and I think that that's the truth of it.

There was a lot of energy expended trying to get me to make the story about Caden looking back on his life at the end, while he's lying in the bed, to change the ending, so it's not about this person, Ellen—who, by the way, may or may not exist. There's no indication that there ever was really an Ellen. Where was she? She never shows up to clean. Caden's inhabiting her for whatever reason. Is his wife fucking with him? Is the world fucking with him? Is Millicent fucking with him? That to me is part of its dreamlike quality. But there is that element of sadness in this real or fictional story that is being told about this woman who's led a very unsatisfying life, and full of regret and loneliness. That mirrors this, even though it's completely different, you know? So, at the end, Caden is apologizing to her mother, who isn't even really her mother because it's an actress who played her mother. And the only human contact, acceptance, and warmth he's gotten in years and years is from an actress who played this fictitious person's mother, but it's enough to make him feel loved. He gets inspired by it, I think. He gets fed and he's able to sort of come alive again for a second. But then he dies.

There's no moment of grace for anybody.
CK: What do you mean by *grace?*

Any moment of inspiration or redemption is immediately undercut, be it forgiveness from Olive or Caden's last second of inspiration. Both are immediately met with die.
CK: It is, but you know what? I think that there's truth in that. That's the other thing about the whole idea of this movie: it's very hard to end a story honestly that doesn't end in somebody's death, because the story isn't over. Movies and books do that all the time, presenting a moment as *the end* but it's not *the end*. The end is always *die*, which gets back to what happens after Hazel dies: then it meanders and doesn't function like a movie structurally would function. People in early screenings wanted the movie to end after he has that night with Hazel. Maybe that's *their* movie, but it's not my movie. I would feel really dishonest ending it there, even if it would make it more popular.

Well, in Adaptation, *Charlie says, "To write about a flower, to dramatize a flower, I have to show the flower's arc. And the flower's arc stretches back to the beginning of life. How did this flower get here? What was its journey? . . . That's what I need to do: tie all of history together."*

CK: Well, you have to. You really have to. And it's true, if you look at any kind of written story. *Adaptation* starts at the beginning of time, and that's really true. I can't tell my story without telling my parents' story, and I can't tell my parents' story without telling their parents' story. Pretty quickly you're at the beginning of time. It's not that far back. And if you believe time doesn't exist and that it's all like a block, what they call the Block Universe Theory, then not only is all *history* part of the story but all *the future* is part of the story, too. You can't say *before* and *after* because there is no before and after.

There's a line in Synecdoche *that "the end is built into the beginning." That seems to play for so much.*

CK: Well, yeah, but it's true. I don't know what to say about that except it's true. You have a relationship that starts; it's going to end. You have a life that started; it's going to end. You don't know how it's going to end, necessarily, but it will end. Of that you can be certain.

Is ending on a resonant moment, then, not enough? An idea that resonates as unresolved, which is Eternal Sunshine, *I think—is that not truthful or a different sort of truthfulness? Or it's just not the whole story?*

CK: You mean the fact that *Eternal Sunshine* ends before the characters die? Yeah, I guess what I could argue in favor of *Eternal Sunshine*, or any story like that, is that you ordinarily have a traditional romantic comedy where they meet each other, they hate each other, they get together, and then they're happy. And that's the end and there is no sense of a life after that, other than they're happy, happy, happy, die. But I think the other kind of honest thing to do is to imply that there is movement after the story is over, and maybe leave uncertain what that movement is. I feel like *Eternal Sunshine* does that. It doesn't say that they're going to be happy, it doesn't say that they're going to be unhappy, but it leaves you with a question: *What is the projection for each of these characters?* And that seems fair to me.

CAST AND CREW CREDITS

SIDNEY KIMMEL ENTERTAINMENT Presents
A LIKELY STORY/
PROJECTIVE TESTING SERVICE/
RUSSIA, INC. Production

SYNECDOCHE, NEW YORK

PHILIP SEYMOUR HOFFMAN   SAMANTHA MORTON
MICHELLE WILLIAMS   CATHERINE KEENER   EMILY WATSON
DIANNE WIEST   JENNIFER JASON LEIGH   HOPE DAVIS   TOM NOONAN

Casting by
JEANNE McCARTHY

Editor
ROBERT FRAZEN

Produced by
ANTHONY BREGMAN
CHARLIE KAUFMAN
SPIKE JONZE

Music Supervisor
BONNIE GREENBERG

Production Designer
MARK FRIEDBERG

Music by
JON BRION

Director of Photography
FREDERICK ELMES, ASC

Produced by
SIDNEY KIMMEL

Visual Effects Supervisor
MARK RUSSELL

Executive Producers
WILLIAM HORBERG
BRUCE TOLL
RAY ANGELIC

Written and Directed by
CHARLIE KAUFMAN

Costume Designer
MELISSA TOTH

CAST
In Order of Appearance

Caden Cotard . . . . . PHILIP SEYMOUR HOFFMAN
Adele Lack . . . . CATHERINE KEENER
Olive (4 years old) . . SADIE GOLDSTEIN
Sammy Barnathan . . . . TOM NOONAN
Emergency Room Doctor . . . . PETER FRIEDMAN
Like Clockwork Patient . . . . CHARLES TECHMAN
Opthalmologist . . . . JOSH PAIS
Tom . . . . DANIEL LONDON
David . . . . ROBERT SEAY
Claire Keen . . . . MICHELLE WILLIAMS
Davis . . . . . STEPHEN ADLY GUIRGIS
Hazel . . . . . . SAMANTHA MORTON
Madeline Gravis . . . . HOPE DAVIS
Plumber . . . . . . FRANK GIRARDEAU
Maria . . . . . JENNIFER JASON LEIGH
Burning House Realtor . . AMY WRIGHT
Derek . . . . PAUL SPARKS
Caden's Father . . . . JERRY ADLER
Caden's Mother . . . . . LYNN COHEN
Ellen's Mother . . DEIRDRE O'CONNELL
Ellen (10 years old) . . . . . KAT PETERS
Dentist . . . . JOHN ROTHMAN
Emergency Room Nurse . . . . AMANDA FULKS
Evaluative Services Doctor . . . . FRANK WOOD
Jazz Singer . . . . DEANNA STOREY
Warehouse Realtor   ELIZABETH MARVEL
Toystore Clerk . . . . LAURA ODEH
Minister . . . . MARK LOTITO
Ariel . . . . DAISY TAHAN
German Woman . . . . ERICA BERG
German Doctor . . . . RAYMOND ANGELIC, SR.
Old Man . . . . . CLIFF CARPENTER
Michael . . . . TIMOTHY DOYLE
Soap Actress Nurse . . . . AMY SPANGER
Soap Actor Doctor . . . . . NICK WYMAN
Therapy Patient Actress . . . . . . PORTIA
Leg Tremor Doctor . . . . . DAN ZISKIE
Lady at Caden's Mom's . . CHRIS McGINN
Adult Olive . . . . . . ROBIN WEIGERT
Man in Line . . . . . GERALD EMERICK
Man with Nose Bleed . . ALVIN EPSTEIN
Frances . . . . . . ROSEMARY MURPHY
Tammy . . . . EMILY WATSON
Needleman Actor . . . . . . TIM GUINEE

Actress Playing Claire . . . KRISTEN BUSH
Actor Playing Needleman Actor
. . . . GREG McFADDEN
Warehouse Actress . . . . BARBARA HAAS
Jimmy . . . . WILLIAM RYALL
Ellen Bascomb/Millicent Weems
. . . . DIANNE WIEST
Maurice . . . . JOE LISI
Actress Playing Frances
. . . . ALICE DRUMMOND
Actor Playing Man with Nose Bleed
. . . . MICHAEL HIGGINS
Actor as Caden . . STANLEY KRAJEWSKI
Medic . . . . TOM GREER
Pastor . . CHRISTOPHER EVAN WELCH
Eric . . . . MICHAEL MEDEIROS

CREW

Unit Production Manager . . RAY ANGELIC
First Assistant Director . . H. H. COOPER
Second Assistant Director
. . . . JENNIFER TRUELOVE

Stunt Coordinator . . . . . . BRIAN SMYJ
Stunt Players . . . . . CHRIS COLOMBO
                        JEFF GIBSON
                        DON HEWITT
                DONALD J. HEWITT, JR.
                        STEPHEN MANN
                        ERIK MARTIN
                        SHAWN O'NEIL
                STEPHANIE STOKES SMYJ
                        PETER THORELL

Production Supervisor . . . . . ERICA KAY

Art Director . . . ADAM STOCKHAUSEN
Set Decorator . . . . . . LYDIA MARKS

Camera Operator . . . LUKASZ JOGALLA
Steadicam Operator/First Assistant Camera
. . . . CARLOS GUERRA
Second Assistant Camera
. . . . SEBASTIAN ALMEIDA
Additional Second Assistant Camera
. . . . ERIC ROBINSON
Motion Control Operator . JAMES RIDER
Motion Control Technician
. . . . DONALD M. CANFIELD
2nd Unit DP/Operator . . DAVID DUNLAP
Stills Photographer . . . ABBOT GENSER
Film Loader . . . . ANNE CARSON

Script Supervisor . . . . MARY CYBULSKI

Sound Mixer . . . . DREW KUNIN
Boom Operator . MARK GOODERMOTE
Cable Puller . . . . . JEANNE GILLILAND

Key Video Assist/Playback Supervisor
. . . . DARREN RYAN
Additional Video Assist
. . . . DEVIN DONEGAN
                        DENNIS GREEN

Production Coordinator
. . . . MARK HAGERMAN
Assistant Production Coordinator
. . . . JAMIE BUCKNER
Production Secretary . . . GARY MARTYN
Production Office Assistants
. . . . MICHAEL BRAUN
                        JOHN EDMUNDSON
                        MATT NICKELSON
                        HENRY PRINCE

2nd 2nd Assistant Director . . NATE GRUBB
Key Set Production Assistant
. . . . MIRASHYAM BLAKESLEE
Set Production Assistants
. . . . ARIANNE APICELLI
                        ADEMOLA McMULLEN
                        MELISSA MESSICK
                        JENNIFER ROBERTS
                        DANA ZOLLI
Additional Set Production Assistants
. . . . JULES HULBURD
                        EVAN SACHS

Assistant Art Director & Storyboard Artist
. . . . KIM JENNINGS
Assistant Art Directors
. . . . DEBORAH JENSEN
                        MARK POLLARD
                LUKE HEGEL-CANTARELLA
Art Department Coordinator
. . . . NORA ASHKAR
Art Department Researcher
. . . . ALEX DIGERLANDO
Art Department Production Assistant
. . . . NICK PALEY
Additional Art Department Assistants
. . . . CHERYL BOYARSKY
                        WILLIAM LOGAN
Graphic Designer . . . . . . ZACH ZIRLIN
Graphics Production Assistant
. . . . PHILIP BUCCELLATO

Assistant Set Decorator
 . . . . . . HEATHER PRENDERGAST
Leadman . . . . TIM METZGER
On Set Dresser . ANTHONY BALDASARE
2nd Dresser . . . . . . ROMAN GRELLER
Set Dressers . . . . . . JOANN ATWOOD
　　　　　　　　　　STEVEN DUKE
　　　　　　　　　JOE TAGLAIRINO
Set Decorating Assistant . . . . HILA KATZ

Property Master . . . SANDY HAMILTON
Assistant Property Master . . KRIS MORAN
2nd Assistant Prop . . . SUSAN PITOCCHI

Lead Greensman . . . . . NICHOLAS HILL
Greensmen . . ALEXANDER BURNHAM
　　　　　　　　　　ARLO HOFFMAN
　　　　　　　　　　RICH LEIBGOLD

Construction Coordinator. . NICK MILLER
Key Shop Craftsman . . GORDON KRAUSE
Key Construction Grip
 . . . . JONATHAN GRAHAM
Foreman Shop Craftsman
 . . . . . . ROBERT A. VACCARIELLO
Best Boy Construction Grip
 . . . . . . TIMOTHY MONTGOMERY

Shop Craftsmen . . . DERRICK ALFORD
　　　　　　　　　　PAUL G. DIVONE
　　　　　　　　　　　HOANG A. LE
　　　　　　　　　PETER MATEJCZYK
　　　　　　　　　　RAYMOND REDDY
　　　　　　　　　　BETSEY TANNER
　　　　　　　　　　JAMES WALKER
　　　　　　　　　BENJAMIN WHITE

Construction Grips . . . . JAMES DEWOLF
　　　　　　　　　　　KEVIN EGAN
　　　　　　　　　　EDWARD EGAN III
　　　　　　　　　　GLEN FJOTLAND
　　　　　　　　　　　JOHN HOUSE
　　　　　　　　　　MELVIN NOPED
　　　　　　　　　　　JAMES REID

Key Construction Electric
 . . . . AMY KUPFERBERG
Charge Scenic . . . . . ELIZABETH LINN
Camera Scenic . . . . . BOB BARNETT
Scenic Foreman . . . . DON NACE
Lead Shop Person . VENAE RODRIGUEZ
Shop Person . . . . . . BRAD BACHTELL
Scenic Artists . . . . . STEPHEN BARTH
　　　　　　　　　　　ABE COSTANZA

Scenic Artists (continued) . . . NIR GAON
　　　　　　　　　　ALISON GILHAM
　　　　　　　　　MELISSA JACKSON
　　　　　　　　　　LISA KENNEDY
　　　　　　　　　　ROB LANDOLL
　　　　　　　　　　NILI LERNER
　　　　　　　　　　HANNAH PRICE

Gaffer . . . . . . JONATHAN LUMLEY
Best Boy Electric . . . . SAM FRIEDMAN
Rigging Gaffer . . . . . . KURT LENNIG
Rigging Best Boy Electric
 . . . . JEFFREY EPLETT
Generator Operator . . MARK VAN ROSSEN
Company Electrics . . . . . . JIM FERRIS
　　　　　　　　　　　TOM LANDI
　　　　　　　　　　JOHN O'MALLEY
　　　　　　　　　　DAVE RUDOLPH
Rigging Electrics . . . . . . JOHN BILLECI
　　　　　TOMAS VON RAUCHHAUPT

Key Grip . . . . BOB ANDRES
Best Boy Grip . . . . . . CHRIS SKUTCH
Dolly Grip . . . . ARTHUR BLUM
Key Rigging Grip . . JACK PANNUCCIO
Rigging Best Boy Grip
 . . . . RICHARD YACUK

Company Grips . . . . ALISON BARTON
　　　　　　　　　　　JOHN BOBICK
　　　　　　　　　BENJAMIN D'ANDREA
　　　　　　　　　　JOHN HALLIGAN
　　　　　　　　　　GRAHAM KLATT
Rigging Grips . . . . . . JOHN FARINA
　　　　　　　　　　PATRICK TAISTRA

Assistant Costume Designer
 . . . . CHRIS ANN PAPPAS
Wardrobe Supervisors . ARLYNN ABSECK
　　　　　　　　　　AMY PICKERING
Key Costumers . . ANGELA MIRABELLA
　　　　　　　　　　CARA CZEKANSKI
Additional Costumer . . MARY GIERCZAK
Costume Production Assistant
 . . . . DIANA PAPPAS

Hair Department Head
 . . . . JERRY DECARLO
Key Hairstylist . . . . . . MANDY LYONS
Wigs Created by
 . . . . MARTIAL CORNEVILLE
　　　　　　　　　　　PAUL HUNTLY
　　　　　　　　　　　PETER OWEN

Makeup Designer . . . . NAOMI DONNE
Prosthetic Makeup Designer
. . . . MIKE MARINO

Makeup Department Head . . JUDY CHIN
Prosthetic Makeup Assistant
. . . . DAVID PRESTO

Olive's Tattoos Designed by . . TIM KERN
Tattoo Transfers Provided by . . . TEMPTU

Prosthetic Renaissance Crew
Art Department. . . . . . PAUL KOMODA
             DAVID FIDEL
             DIANA YOO
Mold Department . . . MIKE ANTOLINO
             CHRIS KELLY
             HAYES VILANDRY
             MIKE MULLIGAN
             MIKE MEASIMER
             STEVE PROUTY
             SHAUNE HARRISON
             CHRIS ARNOLD
             JIMMY RAMONE MARINO
             SCOTT WALLACE
             ANDREA BERGSTOL
             DIANA YOO

Production Accountant . . SEAN HOGAN
First Assistant Accountant
. . . . FRANK MURRAY
Payroll Accountant . . . . . ANNA BOSCO
Second Assistant Accountant
. . . . BRENNAN SHROFF
Post Production Accounting
. . . . STEVE BOYLE, JFA, INC.

Special Effects Coordinator
. . . . DREW JIRITANO
Special Effects Foreman . . . MARK BERO

Location Manager . . . STEVE WEISBERG
Assistant Location Managers
. . . . DAVID GINSBERG
             KIMBERLY FEINMAN
2nd Assistant Location Manager
. . . . KAT DONAHUE
Locations Scouts . . . . CAREY SEWARD
             ERIC PAPA
Locations Assistant . . . . CHRIS CLOUD
Locations Production Assistant . . JESS MAGEE
Parking Coordinator . . . . . JOSE TEJADA

Assistant Parking Coordinator
. . . . DAVID LAURENTIN

Transportation Captains. . . KEVIN KEEFE
             TIMOTHY PAUSTIAN
Transportation Co-Captains
. . . . ROBERT LANSING
             TONY INGRASSELLINO
Drivers. . . . . MATT CALLAGY
             MICHAEL CANALE
             RICH CLARK
             PETER COSTELLO
             TOM CREEHAM
             MARK DOLCE
             KEVIN FLYNN
             JAMES GIBLIN
             CARL HEITTLING
             BRIAN HOGAN
             ROBERT L. JOHNSON
             KRISTOPHER K. KEEFE
             JEREMY OLSZEWSKI
             JOSEPH PAPROTA
             RICHARD PRESUTTI
             MICHAEL RUSSELL
             BIYAMI SIAK
             BILL STUART
             STEVEN TARANTO

POST PRODUCTION

Post Production Supervisor
. . . . JESSICA LEVIN
Assistant Editor . . . . . . BETH MORAN

Supervising Sound Editor/Dialog Editor
. . . . PHILIP STOCKTON
Supervising Sound Editor/Sound Designer
. . . . EUGENE GEARTY

Re-Recording Mixers . . REILLY STEELE
             EUGENE GEARTY
Sound Re-Recordist. . DROR GESCHEIT
Mixed At . . . . SOUND ONE
Dolby Sound Consultant . . DAVID BERTI

Dialog Editors . . . . FRED ROSENBERG
             BRANKA MRKIC-TANA
Foley Supervisor . . . . . FRANK KERN
Foley Editors . . . . KAM CHAN
             JAMIE BAKER
Foley Artist. . . . . MARKO COSTANZO
Foley Mixer. . . . . GEORGE LARA

ADR Editor . . . . RUTH HERNANDEZ
First Assistant Sound Editor
. . . . CHRIS FIELDER
Second Assistant Sound Editor
. . . . DEBORA LILAVOIS
Effects Assistant Editor
. . . . LARRY WINELAND
Apprentice Sound Editor. . JESSICA PARKS
Sound Intern . . . CLÉMENCE STOLOFF
Post Production Sound Facility
. . . . C5 INC., NEW YORK
ELISABETH GIGLIO
DOE KIM

ADR Voice Casting. . BARBARA HARRIS

Special Visual Effects by Brainstorm Digital
Visual Effects Supervisor
. . . . ERIC J. ROBERTSON
Visual Effects Producers
. . . . . . RICHARD FRIEDLANDER
GLENN ALLEN
CG Supervisor . . . . . . BRETT MILLER
Digital Compositors
. . . . CHRIS "PINKUS" WESSELMAN
DANIEL ABRAMOVICH
SCOTT MINTER
ALEKSANDAR DJORDJEVIC
JUN ZHANG
STEWART POMEROY
Matte Artists . . . . . GARRETT EATON
MATTHEW CONNER
Senior Systems Engineer. . . JUSTIN BALL
Operations Manager . . . . GUY BARRESI

Special Visual Effects by Edgeworx
Visual Effects Supervisor and Title Design
. . . . JOHN BAIR
Visual Effects Producer. RENUKA BALLAL
CG Artists . . . . . . CONNIE CONRAD
NATHAN MEIER

Special Visual Effects by Circle-S Studios
Visual Effects Supervisor
. . . . SCOTT FRANKEL
Visual Effects Producer
. . . . PALOMA AÑOVEROS
Digital Artist . . . . . JEREMIAH GRANT

Special Visual Effects by Anibrain, India
VFX Supervisor
. . . . JESH KRISHNA MURTHY
VFX Producer . . . . . ROOPESH GUJAR
VFX Coordinator . . . PREETI SHARMA

Head of Business Development
. . . . MICHAEL S. PRYOR
Compositing Artists . . P NANDAKUMAR
PURTI PITALE
KARUNA MAKHIJA
SUDHIR BANEKAR
VASISTHA CHAWDA
SANDEEP KHEDKAR
RUCHIRA SHARMA
VIJAY S DESHMUKH
K SHRINIWAS
GAURI BHAGWAT
ANKUR SACHDEV
SUJATA S CHOUDHARI
MOHMED GHOUSE
RAHUL D KULKARNI
SUSHIL KALYANSHETTI

Academy of Art University
Compositing Supervisor and Instructor
. . . . CATHERINE TATE
Production Coordinator
. . . . T. PATRICK JOHNSON
Roto/Paint Supervisor and Instructor
. . . . AARON MUSZALSKI
Compositors and Paint/Roto Artists
AARON GERHARD CHIESA
MARC MACHUCA
UTUMPORN CHOMPEN
ANTHONY MESCHI
JESSICA DONNELLY
DANIEL MONISTERE
ERIK GONZALEZ
OLOV SAMUELSSON
IZCHEL C. HUERTA
MAURICIO VALDERRAMA

Technical Assistant . . JEREMY A. PARRISH
Dirt Removal . . . . KARL SISON
Head of Animation and Visual Effects AAU
. . . . CHRIS ARMSTRONG
Computer Lab Manager AAU
. . . . GALINA ROZINA
RotoFactory
VFX Producer . . . . RENE TOUGERON
Digital Effects Lead
. . . . NICHOLAS CERNIGLIA
Digital Artists. . . . . SHUICHI YOSHIDA
JUAN MELGOZA
RADLEY TERUEL
ELOISA HONRADA
STEVE MIHAYLOV
JAMES PINA
SCOTT GAYNOS

Digital Compositors. . . PETER AMANTE
SUE NELSON

Animated Television Sequences by
. . . . KATRINA WHALEN

Visual Effects Coordinator
. . . . PARKER CHEHAK
Visual Effects Assistant
. . . . ALEC STYBORSKI

Digital Intermediate by
. . . . . DELUXE | EFILM | TORONTO

DI Colorist . . . . JOE GAWLER
DI Producers . . . PETER ARMSTRONG
TERRA BLISS
DI Coordinator . . . . LEE HUGHES
DI Editors . . . . JACK LEWARS
DAVE MUSCAT
Digital Opticals . . . CHRIS MACKENZIE
MOTASSEM YOUNES
AHMAD ISMAIL
DI Scanning/Recording NICK PAULOZZA
TREVOR LEWIS
TOM MAYCLIM
Dustbusting . . . . . . STEPHEN BROWN
JAMIE FRANKLIN
TREVOR PICKARD
ALISON SCHOUTEN

Score Produced by . . . . . JON BRION
Supervising Music Editor . . JIM SCHULTZ
Auricle Operator . . . . . . JAY DUERR
Orchestrations by . . . . . . JON BRION
STEVE BARTEK
Music Copyist . . JULIAN BRATOLYUBOV
Score Conducted by . . . . . JON BRION
Orchestra Contractor . . GINA ZIMMITTI
Protools Editing . . . . ERIC CAUDIEUX
Original Score Recorded and Mixed by
. . . . GREG KOLLER
Score Recorded at
. . . . OCEANWAY STUDIOS
Assistant Engineers . . ROUBLE KAPOOR
PATRICK SPAIN
Assistant to Jon Brion
. . . . ASHLEY ARRISON
Additional Musicians
Drums. . . . . JIM KELTNER
Bass. . . . . . SEBASTIAN STEINBERG
Saxophone and Guitar. . . JASON FREESE
Synthesizer . . . . BRET RAUSCH
Gospel Singer. . . . . JIM GILSTRAP

SKE Music Executive
. . . . CHRISTY GERHART

Production Executive for Likely Story
. . . . STEFANIE AZPIAZU

Assistant to Mr. Kaufman
. . . . KATRINA WHALEN
Assistant to Mr. Bregman . . . JULIA BERG
Assistant to Mr. Jonze
. . . . NATALIE FARREY
Assistant to Mr. Horberg
. . . . CHANTAL NONG
Assistant to Mr. Hoffman
. . . . SARA MURPHY

Unit Publicist . . . . . . FRANCES FIORE

Product Placement by . . WENDY COHEN
PRODUCTION RESOURCES

Rights & Clearances by
ENTERTAINMENT CLEARANCES INC
CASSANDRA BARBOUR
LAURA SEVIER

Legal Services
FRANKFURT KURNIT KLEIN & SELZ, P.C.
ALISON S. COHEN
HAMISH BERRY
GABRIELLA LUDLOW

Payroll Service
. . . . . ENTERTAINMENT PARTNERS
Completion Guaranty Provided by
. . . . FILM FINANCES

Dialect Coach . . . CHARLOTTE FLECK

Casting Associates . . NICOLE ABELLERA
RORI BERGMAN
Casting Assistants . . . . JOANNE BLOOM
LESLIE WOO
Extras Casting . . HEATHER REIDENBACH
FOR CENTRAL CASTING
Mr. Hoffman's Stand-In
. . . . SCOTT GLASCOCK
Ms. Morton's Stand-In
. . . . M. AMELIA MARTIN
Ms. Williams's Stand-In
. . . . BERNADETTE YORK
Ms. Keener's Stand-In
. . . . JANELLE TEDESCO

Animals Provided by
. . . . ANIMAL ACTORS, INC.
Animal Trainers . . . . . . KIM KRAFSKY
STEVE McAULIFF

Set Medics . . . . . MAUREEN BEITLER
JONATHAN ELLIS

Catering By
  HENRY'S INTERNATIONAL CUISINE
Chefs. . . . . PETER ANDERS
HENRY PREVIL
Chef Assistant . . JORGE H. CARANGUI
Craft Service By . . . . J&P CRAFT
Head Craft Service . . . JASON ACEVEDO
PETER MARSCHARK
Craft Service Assistants
. . . . GEORGE GRENIER III
TODD KELLY

Interns . . . . CHRISTIAN AMUNDSON
BEN ALTARESCU
EMILY BOETTCHER
GEOFFREY BOOTH
LIA BURKEMAN
INHAN CHO
DYLAN CORRELL
MEGHAN COREA
CHRIS FORESTER-SMITH
EDWARD BURSCH
DAVID FORMENTIN
JESSE KATES
LAURA FINE
MARK HARRISON
JACOB JAFFKE
DAVID MOSHE
DANIEL LAM
OLIVIA VANLEEUWEN
PALOMA MELE
MAYA RUDOLPH
NICK RAY
RONDI SCOTT
SAMANTHA RACANELLI
SEBASTIAN SLAYTER
SHIVA BAJPAI
MARYLOU VETTER
DANIEL SPENCE
POWERS WELDON
ELIZABETH WEISBLATT
HANA YOO
RYAN WESTPHAL
DAVID YOON

"Synecdoche Song"
Written by Charlie Kaufman & Jon Brion
Performed by Sadie Goldstein

"Jingle Bells"
Traditional
Arranged by Jon Brion

"Auld Lang Syne"
Traditional
Arranged by Jon Brion

"Gravity"
Written by Charlie Kaufman and
Deanna Storey
Performed by Deanna Storey

"I'm Just A Little Person"
Written by Charlie Kaufman & Jon Brion
Vocals recorded and engineered by
Juan Patino
Performed by Deanna Storey

"Song For Caden"
Written by Charlie Kaufman & Jon Brion
Vocals recorded and engineered by
Juan Patino
Performed by Deanna Storey

Adele's Paintings by
ALEX KANEVSKY
J. Cacciola Gallery
Dolby Chadwick Gallery
Rosenfeld Gallery

Artwork by Katy Hamer, Courtesy of
the Artist

The Metropolitan Museum of Art,
New York

G. J. Whitrow, "Some Reflections on the
Problem of Memory"
Annals of New York Academy of Sciences,
Blackwell Publishing

Excerpt from "Death of a Salesman"
Courtesy of the
Arthur Miller 2004 Literary and Dramatic
Property Trust

"The New Yorker" Courtesy of Conde Nast
Publications

The U.S. Postal Service Corporate Signature and U.S.Postal Service Retail Clerk Uniform are trademarks of the United States Postal Service and are used with permission.

SPECIAL THANKS
Michael Andreen
Goetz Grossman
Jill Smith
Ingo Maurer
Royal Oak Bar
Art & Industry
The City of Yonkers
Cypress Hills Cemetery
Westchester Film Office
Fire Department of New York
New York City Traffic Control Division
The City of New York Mayor's Office for Film, Theatre, and Broadcasting
Film Commissioner Katherine Oliver
New York State Governor's Office for Motion Picture and Television Development
Executive Director Pat Swinney Kaufman
Deputy Director Jerry Stoeffhaas
Warren Frank
Dustin Hoffman
Aero
Format
Odegard
Luceplan
Cappallini
Kate Spade
Reidel Crystal
Assouline Books
Jacques Carcanagues, Inc.
Property Furniture, NYC
The Yaddo Corporation
The National Park Service
United States Post Office® courtesy of the United States Postal Service®

Cameras provided by ARRIFLEX/Camera Service Center
Chapman Leonard Dollies provided by Panavision New York

American Humane Association monitored the animal action.
No animal was harmed in the making of this film. (AHA 01762)

Originated on KODAK

Color by DELUXE
Prints Released on Kodak
Prints by Deluxe

MPAA Reg No. 44351

The events and characters depicted in the motion picture are fictitious.
Any similarity to actual persons, living or dead, is purely coincidental.

This motion picture is protected under the laws of the United States and other countries. Unauthorized duplication, distribution or exhibition may result in civil liability and criminal prosecution.

© 2008 Kimmel Distribution, LLC.
All Rights Reserved

SKE / LIKELY STORY
/ PROJECTIVE TESTING SERVICE /
RUSSIA INC

About the Screenwriter/Director

CHARLIE KAUFMAN is the writer of the films *Being John Malkovich* (1999), *Human Nature* (2001), *Confessions of a Dangerous Mind* (2002), *Adaptation* (2002), and *Eternal Sunshine of the Spotless Mind* (2004). *Synecdoche, New York* marks Kaufman's film directorial debut.

Initially coming from a background in theater and film, Kaufman has also had a successful run as a TV writer, working on such shows as *Get a Life* and *The Dana Carvey Show*. In 2005, he teamed up with composer Carter Burwell and directors Joel and Ethan Coen to write and direct two "sound plays" for *The Theater of the New Ear* series, staged in Brooklyn, London, and Los Angeles: *Hope Leaves the Theater*, starring Hope Davis, Peter Dinklage, and Meryl Streep; and *Anomalisa*, with David Thewlis, Jennifer Jason Leigh, and Tom Noonan (LA only).